Frances E. Willard

How to Win: A Book for Girls

Frances E. Willard

How to Win: A Book for Girls

ISBN/EAN: 9783743341487

Manufactured in Europe, USA, Canada, Australia, Japa

Cover: Foto ©Lupo / pixelio.de

Manufactured and distributed by brebook publishing software (www.brebook.com)

Frances E. Willard

How to Win: A Book for Girls

HOW TO WIN.

A BOOK FOR GIRLS.

BY

FRANCES E. WILLARD,
President of the National Woman's Christian Temperance Union.

WITH AN INTRODUCTION BY

ROSE ELIZABETH CLEVELAND.

"Be not simply good—be good for something."—THOREAU.

FOURTH EDITION.

FUNK & WAGNALLS, PUBLISHERS.

NEW YORK: 1887.   LONDON:
18 & 20 ASTOR PLACE.   44 FLEET STREET.

Entered, according to Act of Congress, in the year 1896,
By FUNK & WAGNALLS,
In the Office of the Librarian of Congress at Washington, D. C.

TO

ANNA A. GORDON,

HERSELF ONE OF THE NOBLEST TYPES OF AMERICAN YOUNG-
WOMANHOOD,

This Book is Dedicated

AS A LOVING SOUVENIR OF EIGHT YEARS' COMRADESHIP
IN THE WHITE-RIBBON ARMY.

INTRODUCTION.

It is a serious, not to say a solemn thing, in these days, to write a book for girls. He or she who addresses words directly to this class of the community incurs a great responsibility; merits great praise or merits great blame. The time is surely, if slowly, passing when "girls" can be talked to, if talked about, in a flippant and irresponsible manner.

Miss Willard has assumed this responsibility, and she has done it in a serious—often a solemn manner. Whatever the critical or unsympathetic reader may find these pages to lack, she (or he) will never be able to assert that they lack sincerity or earnestness. Miss Willard desires the best things for girls, and for all girls—old girls and young girls —and there is no good girl who reads this book who will not wish hereafter to be a better girl.

Some chapters in this book will excite argument; will provoke contradiction; in short, will do the one best thing a book can do—*set its readers to thinking.*

Rose Elizabeth Cleveland.

CONTENTS.

CHAPTER I.
Why I Wrote of Winning.. 11

CHAPTER II.
"I am Little, but I am I".. 20

CHAPTER III.
Aimless Reverie versus a Resolute Aim—The New Profession... 27

CHAPTER IV.
The New Ideal of Womanhood....................................... 48

CHAPTER V.
The New Ideal of Manhood... 58

CHAPTER VI.
The Beautiful.. 66

CHAPTER VII.
The Decalogue of Natural Law..................................... 76

CHAPTER VIII.
The Law of Habit... 86

CONTENTS.

CHAPTER IX.
How do You Treat Your Laundress?........................ 95

CHAPTER X.
Novel-Reading 102

CHAPTER XI.
Woman's Opportunity in Journalism 105

CHAPTER XII.
At What Age Shall Girls Marry?......................... 117

CHAPTER XIII.
To the Young Women's Christian Temperance Unions—
Unity of Purpose 122

CHAPTER XIV.
"Finally, Sisters" 124

.*. By permission of Rev. Dr. Theodore L. Flood, several chapters originally written for *The Chautauquan* are included in this book.

HOW TO WIN:

A BOOK FOR GIRLS.

CHAPTER I.

WHY I WROTE OF WINNING.

LONG ago, and long ago it was, in the days when I used proudly to write "School Teacher" after my name, I bought a certain book for the express purpose of reading it to the girls I've left behind me. The book is one beloved by train boys, of which they and other venders have sold so many that the latest dodgers read, "Twentieth thousand now in press." It is sensible in matter, attractive in style, and goes by the enticing name of "Getting on in the World." Naturally enough it was written in Chicago, and like most "Garden City" notions, is a success. But the trouble with this volume was that it didn't fill the bill. I wanted to read it to "my girls," to stir up their pure minds by way of remembrance that "life is real, life is earnest," and the rest of it. But as I scanned its bright and pleasant pages I found out—what do you think I found? Why, that with the light of a new dispensation blazing in upon him, and the soprano voices of several million "superfluous women" crying, "Have you no *work* for me to do?" this honored author had written never a word about creation's gentler half! His book contained three hundred and sixty-five pages, but if you had read a page each day, all the year round, you wouldn't have found out at last that such a being as a woman was trying to " to get on" in this or any other world. Not a bread-winning weapon had he put into the hand of the neediest among us, nor had he, even in a stray chapter or " appendix," taken us off by ourselves and drawn us a diagram of our " sphere."

I was so pained by this that I wrote Professor M—— (the gifted author, and my personal friend), asking him why he had thus counted out the women folks in his book upon success in life. I even ventured to hypothecate his reason, saying to him:

"DEAR SIR: I do not think you did this with malice aforethought, or from lack of interest in our fate, but simply and only because, like so many of our excellent brethren, you 'done forgot all about us,' as *Topsy* would say."

Whereupon came a prompt and gracious reply, with the frank admission:

"You guessed aright; I simply forgot to speak of women."

Now, you perceive, it set me thinking—this obliquity of mental vision, which had led a writer so talented and wise to squint thus at the human race, seeing but half of it. I recalled the fact that, into most families, are born girls as well as boys; nay, that, as many an overburdened *pater familias* can testify, girls come not unfrequently in largely superior, if not exclusive numbers. Having, also, at a remote period of my history, belonged to their helpless fraternity, I was haunted by the wish that I might write a sequel to the professor's excellent book, talking therein to girls and women about success in life. Perhaps my time has come — perhaps I have now the largest audience that has yet consented to listen to my "views." Anyhow, I mean, in these off-hand pages, to talk to girls of "How to Win" in something besides the sense treated of in books of etiquette and fashion magazines, or systematically taught in dancing-schools.

And now, my dears, if you are patient and my small assistant keeps me in lead-pencils, I shall try to show that if every young woman held in her firm little hand her own best gift, duly cultivated and made effective, society would not explode, the moon would not be darkened, the sun would still shed light. As things are now, when I see an audience of young men, they remind me of a platoon of soldiers, marching with fixed bayonet to the capture of their destiny, while an assembly of young women, on the other hand, recalls a flock of lambs upon a pleasant hillside, that frisk about and nibble at the herbage and lie down in the sun. Above them soars the devouring eagle of their destiny, sweeping in concentric rings through the blue air, and ready to pounce down upon them, while the meek little innocents turn their white faces skyward and mildly wonder "what that graceful creature is up yonder?" Girls remind me, too, of the reply given by a bright young friend of mine to the solemn exhortation that she should "make the most of life."

"Humph!" she exclaimed, with a rueful grimace,

"I have no chance, for life is busy making the most of me!"

The trouble is, we women have all along been set down on the world's programme for a part quite different from the one we really play upon its stage. For instance, the programme reads: "Woman will take the part of Queen in the Drama of Society," but ofttimes, before the curtain falls, the stage reveals her as a dressmaker, a school teacher—perchance that most abused of mortals—a reformer! The programme reads: "This august actress will be escorted to the stage by Man, her loyal and devoted subject, to whom has been assigned the part of shielding her from the glare of the footlights, and shooting anybody in the audience who dares to hiss." But, alas! ofttimes the stage reveals her coming in alone, dragging her own sewing-machine, while her humble and devoted subject, with tailors' goose in one hand and scissors in the other, indicates by energetic pantomime his fixed intention to drive her speedily behind the scenes. The programme, my beloved innocents, attires you all in purple and fine linen and bids you fare sumptuously every day, but not infrequently the stage reveals you attired in calico gowns, and munching your hard-earned crackers and cheese. The world's theory furnishes every young lady that draws breath, with a lover, loyal and true, but the world's practice shoots him on the battle-field, or stunts and poisons him with alcohol and nicotine, until he can only "rattle around" through life in the place God meant him to fill within home's sacred sanctuary. It is just this discrepancy that I complain of, and the generous age we live in is complaining of it with a thousand tongues, so that the logic of events that happen, rather than the logic of events that ought to happen, is impelling toward nobler fortunes that phenomenal creature whom a French author has called "the Poor Woman of the nineteenth century."

Naturally enough, in thinking over the "Case," I contrast your aims in life with what were once my aims, your outlook upon life with mine. The other day I brought from the vasty deep of the family garret some of my girlish journals, which I was curious to compare with the diary of a friend and former pupil at Evanston. Let me give you a few parallel passages because of the lesson they teach. My pupil (aged sixteen) writes thus:

"Was registered this day a member of the Freshman class in the —— University. The president advises me to take the classical course, and I've made up my mind to try it."

From mine at fifteen years I read:

"Caught a blue jay in my trap out in the hazel thicket. I knew he wasn't 'game' and let him go. The schoolhouse in our district is finished at last. A graduate of Yale College, and former tutor at Oberlin, is to be our teacher. I shall attend regularly, visiting my traps on the way."

Later:

"Sister and I got up long before light to prepare for the first day at school. We put all our books in mother's satchel; had a nice tin pail full of dinner. I study arithmetic, geography, grammar, reading, and spelling, which takes up every minute of my time. Stood next to Pat O'Donahue in spelling, and Pat stood at the head."

From my pupil's diary, a few months later, take this extract:

"I am thinking seriously about my future. Perhaps this is premature, for I am only in my Freshman year, but I have just about decided that I'll study medicine."

From mine, at a similar age (you see precocity was not among my failings):

"Sister was sick, and I brought out all my little bottles of sugar, salt, and flour. Besides these medicines, I dosed her with pimentoes, and poulticed her with cabbage-leaves, but she grew no better, quite fast, so mother called another doctor. Dear me, if I were my brother, instead of being only a girl, we'd soon see whether I've a talent for medicine or not."

From my young friend I quote again:

"I am greatly interested in the question for debate in our literary society this week, especially as I am chief disputant on the affirmative. It reads as follows: *Resolved*, That the votes of women are needed to help put down the liquor traffic."

From mine:

"It is election day and my brother is twenty-one years old. How proud he seemed as he dressed up in his best clothes and drove off with father to vote for John C. Fremont, like the sensible 'Free Soiler' that he is! My sister and I stood at the front window and looked out after them. Somehow I felt a lump in my throat, and then I couldn't see their wagon any more, things looked so blurred. I turned to Mary, and she, dear little innocent, seemed wonderfully sober, too. I said: 'Wouldn't you like to vote as well as Oliver? Don't you and I love the country just as well as he, and doesn't the country need our ballots?' Whereupon she looked scared, but answered: 'Of course we do, but don't you go ahead and say so, for then we should be called strong-minded.'"

From my pupil at seventeen I quote once more:

"The recent articles by members of the 'Women's Congress,' some people would call radical, but they express precisely my opinions on the dress question. It is time for me to assume the garb of a young lady, but upon two things I am determined: First, I will never trail my garments on a filthy pavement while I live. If I am the only young lady in this university who, when she walks, wears walking costume, I will still be true to my individual sense of cleanliness and taste. I will also carry the jewel of an *unpunctured ear* through life, though, by so doing, I oblige Mr. Darwin to confess 'a missing link' between me and my evolutionary ancestors."

Finally, from mine:

"This is my seventeenth birthday, and the date of my martyrdom. Mother insists that at last I *must* have my hair 'done up woman fashion.' She says she can hardly forgive herself for letting me 'run wild' so long. We had a great time over it all, and here I sit, like another Samson, 'shorn of my strength.' That figure won't do, though, for the greatest trouble with me is that I never shall be shorn again! My 'back hair' is twisted up like a corkscrew; I carry eighteen hair-pins; my head aches, my feet are entangled in the skirt of my new gown. I can never jump over a fence again so long as I live. As for chasing the sheep down in the shady pasture, it's out of the question, and to climb to my 'Eagle's Nest' seat in the big burr oak would ruin this new frock beyond repair. Altogether, I recognize the fact that 'my occupation's gone.'"

My readers smile at this, but they may be assured there are such blots upon the page where it was written as briny drops alone can make.

You see, dear friends, from this contrast I have drawn, showing a glimpse of past and future in two eager young lives, how fast this world is getting on. What is the difference in the outlook of your life that is and mine that used to be? Let us consider: I was a daring sort of girl; you are the sort of girls who dare. I had aspiration; you have opportunity. I breathed an atmosphere laden with old-time conservatisms, from which my glorious mother's liberality of soul was my one safety-valve of deliverance; you are exhilarated by the vital air of a new liberty. "The world is all before you, where to choose." If I required but little of myself, it was because the world required so little of me. No college of first rank in East or West—save noble old Oberlin and generous Antioch—could have been coaxed to count me in when she made up her jewels. Briefly, public opinion proposes to give you a chance. It proposed to let me shirk for myself. It means to put a shield in your left hand and a sword in your right. It let me go forth, as best I could, to beat the air with unarmed hands, or to sharpen my weapons on the field and in plain sight of the enemy.

Society set before me very few incentives, and commended to me only the passive virtues. Indeed, she never really bestirred herself on my behalf at all, save that she ceased not in story and poem, by sermon and song, by precept and example, and (most cogently of all) by setting no other hope before me, to ground me, so far as she was able, in the philosophy that sustained the illustrious Micawber.

"Now, my daughter," thus was she won't to speak, "do you but be docile and obedient, as a young woman should, and something—something very particular, indeed—will most assuredly turn up."

But I learned early to distrust a Mentor who took so little cognizance of the imperious ardor of my youth; who was so stupidly oblivious of the varied possibilities in brain and hand and heart, and so I began early to follow out my own devices as to a plan of character and work. Would that the generous impulse of your enthusiasm, guided by your broader opportunity, might

> "Give me back the wild pulsation
> That I felt before the strife,
> When I heard my days before me,
> And the tumult of my life."

CHAPTER II.

"I AM LITTLE, BUT I AM I."

WITH the Past for a background, I have tried to picture the opportunity which the Present holds up before the daughters of America. Let me now, for a brief space, coming freshly from the field of active service, try to talk about the conditions of success in this wonderful battle of life. First, then, I would give this not at all startling bit of advice: *Keep to your specialty;* to the doing of the thing that you accomplish with most of satisfaction to yourself, and most of benefit to those about you. Keep to this, whether it be raising turnips or tunes; painting screens or battle-pieces; studying political economy or domestic receipts; for, as we read in a great author who has a genius for common sense: "There is not one thing that men ought to do, there is not one thing that ought to be done, which a woman ought not to be encouraged to do, if she has the capacity for doing it. For wherever there is a gift, there is a prophecy pointing to its use, *and a silent command of God to use it.*" Such utterances as these are assertions of the " natural and inalienable rights" of the *individual* as such. They are deductions of the Christian philosophy which regards you and me, first and chiefly, as human beings, and makes the greatest possible account of personal identity.

In all ages there have been minds that saw this truth. The intellects which towered like Alpine peaks above the mass of men were the first to reflect its blessed light. Two thousand years ago, Juvenal made the heroine of a famous "Satire" say to the hero: "I like our Latin word for *man*, which equally includes your sex and mine. For you should not forget that, in all things highest, best, and most enduring in our natures, I am as much a man as you are." The sun of truth looms high above the far horizon in our day, and even the plains of human thought and purpose are glowing with the light of this new inspiration. "Personal value," "personal development," these will be the noontide watchwords, "when the race out of childhood has grown." Only yesterday I heard a fashionable butterfly, in the surroundings of a luxurious home, saying with sudden enthusiasm: "Of one thing I am sure ; every woman that lives is bound to find out what is the very best thing she can do with her powers, and then she's bound to do it." In creating each of us with some peculiar talent, God has given us each "a call" to some peculiar work. Indeed, the time is almost here when the only call that will be recognized as valid, in any field, must involve in him who thinks he hears it both adaptation and success. Each one of us is a marvellous bundle of aptitudes and of capacities. But, just as I prefer the active to the passive voice, I prefer to put the aptitudes first in my present inventory. Besides, the world has harangued us women on our capacities, from the beginning, and it is really refreshing to take the dilemma of our destiny by the other horn, at last ! Civilization (by which I mean Christianity's effect on the brains and hands of humanity) wonderfully develops and differentiates our powers.

Among the Modocs there are but four specialties—assigned with remarkable fairness, in the proportion of two for the squaws and two for the braves. The last hunt and fight; the first do the drudgery and bring up the pappooses. Among the Parisians, on the contrary, the division of labor is almost infinite, so that the hand perfectly skilled in the most minute industry (as, for instance, in moulding the shoestrings of a porcelain statuette) needs no other resource to gain a comfortable livelihood. Among the Modocs, skins are about the only article of commerce. Among the Parisians, evolution has gone so far in the direction of separating employments formerly blended, that you cannot buy cream and milk in the same shop.

By some unaccountable perversion of good sense, the specialties of human beings who are women have been strangely circumscribed. But they were *there*, all the same, and now, under the genial sun of a more enlightened era, they are coming airily forth, like singing-birds after a thunder-storm, and wonderfully do they help some of us to solve the toughest of all problems: *What is life for?*

Let us see. Lift the cover of your sewing-basket: there are thimble, scissors, spools of thread, and all the neat outfit needful to a seamstress, but minus the needle they have no explanation and no efficiency. Unlock your writing-desk: what are paper, ink, and sealing-wax, without the pen? They are nothing but waste material and toys. So it is with you and me. We have no explanation that is adequate; we have no place in the work-box and portfolio of to-day; no place in the great humming hive of the land we live in, save as some predominating aptitude in each of us explains why we are here, and in what way we are to swell the inspiring song of voluntary toil and beneficent success. Suppose that here and now, you proceed to take an "inventory of stock," if you have not been thoughtful enough to do that already. Made up as you are, what is your *forte*, your "specialty," your "best hold," as men phrase it? Be sure of one thing, at the outset: The great Artificer, in putting together your individual nature, did not forget this crowning gift, any more than He forgets to add its own peculiar fragrance to the arbutus, or its own song to the lark. It may not lie upon the surface, this choicest of your treasures; diamonds seldom do. Miners lift a great deal of mere dust before the sparkling jewel they are seeking gladdens the eye. Genius has been often and variously defined. I would call it *an intuition* of one's own best gift. Rosa Bonheur knew hers; Charlotte Cushman recognized hers; George Eliot was not greatly at a loss concerning hers. As for us, of less emphatic individuality, sometimes we wait until a friend's hand leads us up before the mirror of our potential self; sometimes we see it reflected in another's success (as the eaglet, among the flock of geese, first learned that he could fly, when he recognized a mate in the heaven-soaring eagle, whose shadow frightened all the geese away); sometimes we come upon our heritage unwittingly, as Diana found Endymion, but always it is there, be sure of that, and "let no man take thy crown." As iron filings fall into line around a magnet, so make your opportunities cluster close about your magic gift. In a land so generous as ours, this can be done by every woman who reads these lines. A sharpened perception of their own possibilities is far more needed by "our girls" than better means for education. But how was it in the past? If there is one reflection which, for humanity's sake, grieves me as no other can, it is this thought of God's endowment bestowed upon each one of us, so that we might in some especial manner gladden and bless the world, by bestowing upon it our best; the thought of His patience all through the years, as He has gone on hewing out the myriad souls of a wayward race, that they might be lively stones in the temple of use and of achievement, and side by side with this the thought of our individual blindness, our failure to discern the riches of brain, heart, and hand, with which we were endowed. But most of all, I think about the gentle women who have lived and died, and made no sign of their best gifts, but whose achievements of voice and pen, of brush and chisel, of noble statesmanship and great-hearted philanthropy, might have blessed and soothed our race through these six thousand years.

There is a stern old gentleman of my acquaintance who, if he had heard what I have felt called upon to say, would have entered his demurrer in this fashion: "That's all fol-de-rol, my friend; a mere rhetorical flourish. If women could have done all this, why didn't they, pray tell? If it's in it's in, and will come out, but what's wanting can't be numbered. You can't pull the wool over my eyes with your vague generalities. I went to the Centennial: I saw Machinery Hall, and what's more for my argument (and less for yours), I saw the 'Woman's Pavilion,' too."

He would then proceed to ask me, with some asperity, if I thought that any of my "gentle myriads" could have invented a steam-engine? Whereupon I would say to him, what I now say to you, "Most assuredly I think so; why not?" And I would ask, in turn, if my old friend had studied history with reference to the principle that, as a rule, human beings do not rise above the standard implied in society's general estimate of the class to which they belong. Take the nations of Eastern Europe and Western Asia; "civilized" nations, too, be it remembered; study the mechanic of Jerusalem, the merchant of Damascus and Ispahan; in what particular are the tools of the one or the facilities of commerce familiar to the others, superior to those of a thousand years ago? Surely, so far as Oriental inventions are concerned, they have changed as little as the methods of the bee or the wing-stroke of the swallow. We hear no more of man's inventiveness in those countries than of woman's. Why should we, indeed, when we remember that both are alike untaught in the arts and sciences which form the basis of mechanical invention? They are inspired by no intellectual movement; no demand; no "modern spirit." It is not "in the air" that *men* shall be fertile of brain and skilled of hand as inventors there, any more than it is here that women shall be, and where both knowledge and incentive are not present, achievement is evermore a minus quantity. None but a Heaven-sent genius, stimulated by a love of science, prepared by special education and inspired by the *prestige* of belonging to the dominant sex, ever yet carved types, tamed lightning or imprisoned steam. Besides, in ages past, if some brave soul, man or woman, conscious of splendid powers, strove to bless the world by their free exercise, what dangers were involved! Was it Joan of Arc? the fagot soon became her portion; or Galileo? on came the rack; or Christopher

Columbus? the long disdain of courtiers and jealousy of ambitious coadjutors followed him; or Stephenson? his fetter was the menace of the law; or Robert Fulton? he faced the sarcasm of the learned and the merriment of boors. Even for the most adventurous inventor of to-day (as the aëronaut experimenters), what have we but bad puns and insipid conundrums, until he wins, and then ready caps tossed high in air and fame's loud trumpet at his ear—when death's cold finger has closed it up forever.

Times are changing, though. The world grows slowly better and more brotherly. The day is near when women will lack no high incentive to the best results in every branch of intellectual endeavor and skilled workmanship. Not a week passes but from the Patent Office comes some favorable verdict as to woman's inventive power. Wisdom's goddess deems herself no longer compromised because places are assigned us in her banquet hall, and I, for one, appeal from the "Woman's Pavilion" of the first, to that which shall illustrate the second hundred years of this Republic.

CHAPTER III.

AIMLESS REVERIE VERSUS A RESOLUTE AIM—THE NEW PROFESSION.

But—as I was saying when the stern old gentleman was pleased to interrupt me—I am to give you reasons why you are to cultivate your specialty. And I claim, first (as has been implied already), that you should do this because you have a specialty to cultivate. (This, on the principle of the old cook-book, which begins its "Recipe for Broiling Hares" with the straightforward exhortation: "First catch your hare.") The second reason is, because you will then work more easily and naturally, with the least friction, with the greatest pleasure to yourself, and the most advantage to those around you. "Paddle your own canoe," but paddle it right out into the swift, sure current of your strongest, noblest inclination. Thirdly, by this means you will get into your cranium, *in place of aimless reverie, a resolute aim*. This is where your brother has had his chief intellectual advantage over you. Quicker of wit than he, far less unwieldy in your mental processes, swifter in judgment, and every whit as accurate, you still have felt, when measuring intellectual swords with him, that yours was in your left hand, that his was in his right; and you have felt this chiefly, as I believe, because from the dawn of thought in his sturdy young brain, he has been taught that he must have a definite aim in life if he ever meant to swell the ranks of the somebodies upon this planet, while you have been just as sedulously taught that the handsome prince might whirl past your door " 'most any day," lift you to a seat beside him in his golden chariot and carry you off to his castle in Spain.

And of course you dream about all this; why shouldn't you? Who wouldn't? But, my dear girls, dreaming is the poorest of all grindstones on which to sharpen one's wits. And to my thinking, the rust of woman's intellect, the canker of her heart, the "worm i' the bud" of her noblest possibilities has been this aimless reverie; this rambling of the thoughts; this vagueness, which when it is finished is vacuity. Let us turn our gaze inward, those of us who are not thoroughgoing workers with brain or hand. What do we find? A mild chaos; a glimmering nebula of fancies; an insipid brain-soup where a few lumps of thought swim in a watery gravy of dreams, and, as nothing can come of nothing, what wonder if no brilliancy of achievement promises to flood our future with its light? Few women, growing up under the present order of things, can claim complete exemption from this grave intellectual infirmity.

Somehow one falls so readily into a sort of mental indolence; one's thoughts flow onward in a pleasant, gurgling stream, a sort of intellectual lullaby, coming no-whence, going no-whither. Only one thing can help you if you are in this extremity, and that is what your brothers have—the snag of a fixed purpose in this stream of thought. Around it will soon cluster the dormant ideas, hopes, and possibilities that have thus far floated at random. The first one in the idle stream of my life was the purpose, lodged there by my life's best friend, my mother, to have an education. Then, later on, Charlotte Brontë's "Shirley" was a tremendous snag in the stream to me. Around that brave and steadfast character clustered a thousand new resolves. I was never quite so steeped in reveries again, though my temptations were unusual; my "Forest Home," by a Wisconsin river, offering few reminders to my girlish thought, of the wide, wide world and its sore need of workers. The next jog that I got was from the intellectual attrition of a gifted and scholarly woman who asked me often to her home and sent me away laden with volumes of Wordsworth, Niebuhr, and the British essayists, not forgetting Carlyle and Emerson. Margaret Fuller Ossoli was another fixed point—shall I not rather say a fixed star? —in the sky of my thought, while Arnold of Rugby, to one who meant to make teaching a profession, was chief of all. Well, is it possible that any word I have here written may set some of you thinking—that's it, *set* you, a fixed purpose rather than a floating one—about a definite object in life toward which, henceforth, you may bend a steady, earnest gaze? I am not speaking of a thorough intellectual training only. It is to the life-work, which only a lifetime can fully compass, that I would direct your thoughts. Rather than that you should fail to have a fixed purpose concerning it, I would that your mental attitude might be like the one confided to me by a charming Philadelphia girl, whose letter of this morning has the following *naïve* statement:

"I feel such an aching in me to do or be something uncommon, and yet a kind of awful assurance that I never shall."

Nor do I here refer to that general knowledge of household arts which forms the sole acquirement inculcated in the regulation "Women's Department" of the bygone-age newspaper, which in many localities remains in this, like the boulder of a past epoch.

It was once thought to be a high virtue for women, no matter how lofty in station or how ample of fortune, to do their own work with the needle. Homer represents Penelope spinning, surrounded by her maids, and classic art abounds with illustrations of like character. But the virtues of one age often become the mistakes of the next. When loom, needle and broom were woman's only weapons, she did well to handle them deftly, no matter what her rank, for they were her bread-winning implements, and fortune has been proverbially fickle in all ages. But men, by their witty inventions, have perpetually encroached on "woman's sphere."

Eli Whitney, with his cotton-gin, Elias Howe, with his sewing-machine, and a hundred other intricate-brained mechanics who have set steel fingers to do in an hour what women's fingers could not accomplish in a year; all these have combined to revolutionize the daily cares of the gentler sex. With former occupations gone, and the world's welcome ready when they succeed in special vocations new to them, it becomes not only the privilege but the sacred duty of every woman to cultivate and utilize her *highest* gift. There is no more practical form of philanthropy than this, for every one who makes a place for herself "higher up" leaves one lower down for some other woman who, but for the vacancy thus afforded her in the world's close-crowded ranks, might be tempted into paths of sin. There is an army of poor girls wholly dependent for a livelihood upon the doing of house-work. They have no other earthly resource between them and the poor-house or haunt of infamy. There is another class to whom an honorable support can come only by sewing or millinery work. Whoever, then, fitting herself for some employment involving better pay and higher social recognition, graduates out of these lower grades and leaves them to those who cannot so advance, has helped the world along in a substantial way, because she has added to the sum of humanity's well-being.

To young women in wealthy homes, these considerations should come with even greater convincing force. As David Swing has wisely said to his own rich congregation:

"The rhetoric thrown at women of property for not doing 'their own work' could only be useful in an age of fashionable idleness, but in a busy age it is a part of nature's law that what are called the 'better classes' shall leave for the poorer classes some labor to be done, just as the Mosaic law left some sheaves in the field for the gleaner. The world's work is to be apportioned according to the need and capability of its workers, and the higher order of power must not encroach upon the task which nature seems to have set apart for the employment and support of the less capable."

Let it not be concluded that I have meant to speak lightly of the intricate, skilled labor involved in making healthful and attractive that bright, consummate flower of a Christian civilization—the home. I have felt that this theme has been so often treated that it needed no amplification at my hands, but I will add that, having been entertained in scores of homes belonging to "exceptional women," "women with a career," etc., my testimony is that for wholesomeness, heartsomeness, and every quality that superadds home-making to housekeeping, I have never seen their superiors, and seldom, take them all in all, their peers. But as a rule, these women have earned the "wherewithal" to make a home, by the exercise of some good gift of brain or hand, and thus having been enabled to put a proxy in the kitchen, they direct, but do not attend personally to the minutiæ of daily household cares.

Cultivate, then, your specialty, because the independence thus involved will lift you above the world's pity to the level of its respect, perchance its honor. Understand this first, last, and always : *The world wants the best thing.* It wants your best. It needs you as a significant figure to give its ciphers value ; to designate as an example ; to serve up in a eulogy, perchance to shine in the galaxy by whose light alone its centuries maintain their places in the firmament of history. I know this may strike you as contradiction, for the paradox of paradoxes is this crotchety but kind, narrow-minded but just old world in which you and I are cast away, like Æneas in the domain of Dido. The effrontery of "Madam Grundy" passes all comprehension, and would be laughable if it were not so sad. She tells us women distinctly that we positively shall not do for society the thing we can do best ; she declares that if we attempt it we shall be frowned down, and practically ostracized, if not utterly made away with, and then, if we go right on and succeed, she trumpets our names from sea to shore, showers us with greenbacks, and nods her conventional old head with a knowing " I told you so." And, *per contra*, while on one hand this same unreasonable old lady cripples our attempts to succeed, on the other she snubs us for not doing that very thing. In fact, she is so poor a mathematician that she has never yet so much as tried to learn the value of the "unknown quantity." The mute Milton is, to her, indeed "inglorious." Her code of ethics recognizes just one crime (not mentioned in the Decalogue), and it is Failure. Her law is written on a single table—it is a table of stone—and it reads thus: "Succeed and live; make shipwreck of success, and die."

And so, young friends, fold away your talents in a napkin if you choose; the world will not openly reprove you. She will never urge you to bring out your hidden treasure, but she knows right well when you defraud her, and the relentless old tyrant will punish you with tireless lash because you did not bring all your tithes into the storehouse of the common good, because you lived "beneath your privilege;" because, for yourself (which means for *her*), you did not "covet earnestly the best gifts." She will cut you on the public street when she would have shown you all her teeth in smiles. She will send poverty on your track, when you might have sat down at her banquet an honored guest. Yes, the world wants the best thing; *your best*, and she will smite you stealthily if you do not hand over your gift. Now, last, but not least (under the head of reasons for seeking to know your true vocation as a human being), let me bring forward the *rationale* of the bread-and-butter argument. In sooth, no writer or speaker may omit it with impunity, if he would retire in good order from an American audience. Briefly, then, your specialty, well trained, is your best bread-winning implement, and she who earliest grasps this, and who firmest holds it, comes off best in the race. "Be not simply good, be good for something," said Henry D. Thoreau. A bright-eyed girl of eighteen used to come to me on Friday evenings to give me German lessons. To be sure, I have lived in Germany, and she has never been out of Illinois, but then that language is not my specialty, while it is hers. "How is it that though so young, you have made yourself independent?" I inquired of her one day. Listen to the reply: "My mother was always quoting this saying of Carlyle: 'The man who has a sixpence commands the world—to the extent of that sixpence.' I early laid this sentiment to heart. Besides, when I was fifteen years old, I heard a sermon on the text: 'This one thing I do.' Being of a practical turn of mind, I made an application of which the preacher, perhaps, had no intention. I thought, why not in every-day affairs as well as in religion do one thing well, rather than many things indifferently, and in that way secure the magic sixpence of Carlyle! My father was a rich man then, but I resolved to prepare myself to teach the German language, of which I was very fond, by way of a profession. When the Chicago fire came we lost our property, but I discovered that I could not only support myself, but help my father to many a convenient sixpence, because in prosperous days I had fore-armed myself with a cultivated specialty."

As she told me this, I thought how, from widely different premises and conditions in life, young people may reach similar conclusions. For instance, on the top of the great St. Bernard, I said to the "Hospitable Father," a noble young monk, "How is it that you, so gifted and well taught, are spending your life away up here among eternal snows?" And I shall never forget his look of exaltation as he simply answered: " 'Tis my vocation—*voilà!*"

After all, this is the vital question: With what sort of a weapon will you ward off the attacks of the blood-hound Poverty, which Dame Fortune is pretty sure to set on everybody's track sooner or later, that she may try his mettle, and learn what manner of spirit he is of? In times like these, when men's hearts are failing them for fear, when riches are saved the trouble of "taking to themselves wings" by the faithless cashiers and book-keepers who are adepts at furnishing these flying implements, and, above all, when labor is coming to be king, the question " *What will you do?*" has fresh significance. Remember, going forth from the uncertain Eden of your dreams, into the satisfying pleasures of honest, hard work, "the world is all before you where to choose." Will you share some other woman's home, and help her make it beautiful? No task more noble or more needed awaits the thoughtful worker of to-day. The world exists but for the sake of its homes. Will you bestow your hand upon some fine æsthetic industry, as drawing, designing, engraving, photographing? Will you telephone or telegraph? Will you be an architect? a printer? an editor? Will you enter one of the three learned professions? Braver women than you or I have won a foothold for us in each of them; as to the brainhold, that is our affair. I will not now pursue the question further. Only Miss Penny's "Cyclopædia of Woman's Occupations" (a book I recommend to your attention) can exhaust it, and with it exhaust you and the world's work, too, for that matter!

After all, it doesn't so much signify what you may do as

that you do it well, whatever it may be. For the value of skilled labor is estimated on a democratic basis, nowadays. President Eliot, of Harvard University, the cook in the Parker House restaurant, and Mary L. Booth, who edits *Harper's Bazar*, each receives $4000 per year.

Think a moment. Will you be led to say, "The good old ways are good enough for me," and so drop into the swollen ranks of teacherdom, or rattle awhile on a martyrized piano, and then set up for a musician, though you have not a particle of music in throat or finger-tips? Or will you stay at home and let papa support you until you grow tired of doing nothing and expecting nothing, and proceed to marry some man whom you endure rather than love, just to get decently out of your dilemma?

Nay, I do you injustice. Few girls who breathe the free air of our Eastern mountains and Western prairies will be so cowardly. I may not construct your horoscope, but this much I will venture—that when you marry, no matter what you *find*, you will *seek* not a name, behind which to cover up the insignificance of your own; not a "good provider," to feed and clothe one who has learned how to feed and clothe herself; not a "natural protector," to shield you in his plaidie, the gallant, gallant laddie, from the cauld, cauld blast; but you will seek (and may Heaven grant that you shall find) that rarest, choicest, most elusive prize of man's existence, as of woman's; one which—mournfully I say it—the modern marriage is by no means certain to involve—namely, *a mate*. At this juncture, shrewd *mater familias* whispers to *pater:* "That's the first orthodox word she's said." Some youth throws down my book and mutters to himself, "There, I knew it would all come to this! Look at the absurdity of these women! Why, they preach up all sorts of trades and professions, and then they come back, at last, to the 'good old way' they have forsaken, and advise every young lady to get a situation in a school of one scholar, and her board thrown in."

Meanwhile, heroic Hypatia sits near by, and "musing in maiden meditation, fancy free," on a "career," murmurs within herself, "To this complexion must it come at last!"

Peace, peace, good friends! This seeming inconsistency is readily explained. In this century, when the wage of battle has cost our land an army of her sons, when widows mourn, and unwedded thousands are forced to meet the hard-faced world (from which rose-water theorists would shield them), America is coming to the rescue of her daughters! For the nearer perfect—that is, the more Christian—a civilization has become, the more carefully are the *exceptional* classes of society provided for. All our philanthropic institutions under State or private patronage illustrate this. In less enlightened days, your ideal woman composed the single, grand class for which public prejudice set itself to provide. She was to be the wife and mother, and she was carefully enshrined at home. But, happily, this is the world's way no longer. The exceptions are so many, made by war, by the thousand misunderstandings and cross-purposes of social intercourse, by the peculiar features of the transition period in which we live, by the absurdly extravagant customs of our day, and the false notions of both men and women—that not to provide for those exceptions would be a monstrous meanness, if not a crime. And the provision made in this instance is the most rational—indeed, the only rational one which it is in

the power of society or government to make for any save
the utterly incapable—namely : *a fair chance for self-help.*
Nor (to pursue the line of our argument still further) can
we forget that skeleton hand which, in utter disregard of
"the proprieties" in destiny's weird drama, thrusts itself
so often into the charmed domestic circle, and snatches the
beloved "provider" away forever, while it sets gaunt
famine by the fireside in his stead. Furthermore can we
forget that, in ten thousand families, wives are this moment
waiting in suspense and agony the return of wretched hus-
bands to homes made hideous by the drunkard's sin—wives
whose work of brain or hand alone keeps their children
from want, now that their "strong staff is broken, and their
beautiful rod." There are delicate white fingers turning
the page on which I print these words, that will never wear
the marriage ring ; there are slight forms bending over my
friendly lines, which, not far down the years, will be
clothed in widow's weeds. Alas, there are as surely others,
who, when they have been wooed and won, shall find that
they are worse than widowed. And what of these three
classes of women, sweet and helpless ? Clearly, to all of
them I am declaring a true and blessed gospel, in this good
news concerning honest independence and brave self-help !
Clearly, also, no one is wise enough to go through the assembly of my readers, and tell us who, in future years,
shall need a bread-winning weapon with which to defend
herself and perchance also the helpless ones between whom
and the world there may be no arm but hers. But it is a
principle in public as well as private economy, that *the
wisest foresight provides for the remotest contingency*, and
thus, in its full force, all that I have been saying applies

to every woman who may read these thoughts on "How to Win." Suppose that many of you, dear girls, are destined to a downy nest, instead of a strong-winged flight—what then ? Will the years spent in making the most of the best powers with which God has endowed you be worse employed than if you had given them to fashion and frivolity ? Those "*ad interim*" years which separate the graduate's diploma from the bride's marriage certificate, can they possibly be invested better than in the acquisition of some useful trade or dignified profession ? And then, aside from this, I would help the youngest of you to remember (even in the bewildered years of her second decade) what noble Margaret Fuller said : "No woman can give her hand with dignity, or her heart with loyalty, until she has learned *how to stand alone.*" It is not so much *what comes to you* as *what you come to*, that determines whether you are a winner in the great race of life. Never forget that the only indestructible material in destiny's fierce crucible is *character*. Say this, not to another—say it to yourself ; utter it early, and repeat it often : *Fail me not, thou.*

Thus far I have been trying to impress upon you the reasons why you should cultivate individuality and independence in word and deed. I have claimed that each one of you has a "call" to some specific work, indicated by God's gifts to you of brain, or heart, or hand. But I would not have you only, or indeed chiefly, concerned with the evolution of your powers for your own sake. If you acquire, let it be that you may dispense ; if you achieve, that others may sun themselves in the kind glow of your prosperity. The people who spend all their strength in absorbing are failures and parasites. It is alike the business of the sun and of the soul to radiate every particle of light that they contain. There is every reason to believe that this is precisely what they are for. And so, having made sure of your light, strength and discipline, strike out from the warm and radiant centre of a self-poised brain and heart, into the lives about you, and you will find that "What is good for the hive is also good for the bee." The luminous characters of history have done this, always. Losing their lives in those of other men, they have found them on the crest of the world's gratitude and fame. What they have done on a grand scale, we, from identical motives, may do on a small one. Such natures are as different from those who cultivate their choicest gift simply for their own sake, as a *lighthouse* is different from a *dark lantern*. "Self-culture" is much in vogue nowadays, and has for its high-priests some of the most incisive minds of this or any age. But self-culture stops in the middle of the sentence I would fain help you to utter. It says: "Make the most of your powers;" it does not say "*for others' sake* as well as for your own." It claims that if we set the candle of our gifts upon the candlestick of modern society, its light will inevitably radiate according to its power of shining, and thus while brightening ourselves we shall have done our utmost toward lighting up the general gloom. But self-culture forgets that a candle is no type of you and me. We are human spirit-lamps, whose rays should be directed and intensified by the blow-pipe of an unceasing purpose; for we are all so made that unless we *will* to light up other lives, we can never do so to the limit of our power. Self-culture is never base; it is often noble, but it can never be the noblest aim of all.

Why is the memory of Mrs. Browning loved beyond that of almost any poet who has sung? Because "the cry of the human" is so strong in that wondrous voice of hers. Why is the name carved deepest on the republic's heart that of its martyr President? Because he lived and toiled for his people's sake, "with malice toward none, with charity for all." Why was the lamentation well-nigh universal when under the sea flashed the telegraphic message, "John Stuart Mill is dead?" Because this quiet thinker lived for other men; because he "struck out from the centre," from himself, that pitiful pivot on which so many human windmills turn, and measured, in the swift flight of his benignant thought, the long radius between himself and the remotest circle of human need; because, more than any other philosopher of his day, he labored for the time when "all men's weal shall be each man's care."

Nay, while I mourn, as I have seldom mourned for an historic character, the cloud that early dimmed, for Stuart Mill, the Star of Bethlehem, I will not, as a woman, withhold from his splendid memory the tribute of my humble gratitude. But while I speak of all these lives, shining like beacon lights of our own day, I would not fail to point you in conclusion toward a wide-armed cross upon a lonely hillside, while I repeat His words who said, "And I, if I be lifted up, will draw all men unto me." Dear girls, CHRIST is the magnet of humanity, and she has found the best vocation, and the highest, who brings most souls diseased within the healing power of His immortal Gospel. This is a work for which women have gifts pre-eminent. The Saxon word for lady means "a giver of bread," and is full of beautiful significance, but America's new century shall evolve another meaning, freighted with greater blessing for humanity: lady, giver of the bread of life! In later years we have had a revelation of our duty to the ungospelled masses, to the "elbow heathen," as an evangelist has called them, to the intemperate (who, as a rule, are quite beyond the hearing of the pulpit's voice), and to the dusky dwellers in the Zenana, whose faces are misty with the unshed tears of generations passed in misery and shame. Two thirds of the Church of Christ are women. By the freer life and richer opportunity which you and I enjoy; by society's growing tolerance, not to say its kindly appreciation, of our activities; by the heart transformed and the peace imparted through the Gospel, the voice of our Redeemer pleads for our consecrated service. I would not undervalue the culture of the intellect, but would exalt the culture of the heart.

Just here let me add a personal appeal based on all that has preceded it, for the line of work that I deem most attractive and most urgently demanded by the exigencies of our time. It is that new and magnificent profession for women, now being brought to almost scientific accuracy and completeness—viz., PHILANTHROPY.

To Young Women who are Ready for Work: The memory of my own early aspirations leads me to address you. I desired financial independence—that is, to bear my own weight; said with Archimedes, "Grant me a place to stand," and sought a lever by which I might help to move the world. If this describes your mental outlook, let us confer together concerning your vocation. There is none nobler than that of a teacher or a professor in an institution for the higher education. But these ranks are overcrowded, and without decided talent, some experience or rare influence, you risk much in making choice of teaching as your field of labor.

Journalism is difficult. Literature, without the highest order of talent, is hopeless. Lyceum lecturing has passed its prime and the most gifted and famous alone can win in that arduous field. Public reading as an avocation for women is as much overcrowded as the legal profession is for men. In music, vocal and instrumental, there is an absolute glut of the market, save for the highly endowed. Moreover, in all these lines the standard is rising so steadily and to such a height that mediocrity, once endurable, is now hopelessly condemned. To be a fourth or even a third-rate musician is to have failed outright. To paint daubs and call them pictures is a positive sin. To murder the modern languages by false accent and atrocious grammar hath not forgiveness in this world. But behold, all these things are done daily by droves of young persons who are blindly or ignorantly resolved upon the unattainable.

The inventory I have outlined includes most of the higher occupations open to women, save one, and that is the broad, nay, the well-nigh boundless field of practical philanthropy. There is a welcome from the best, for women, on the moral battlefields of this busy age. Soldiers are needed; new recruits eagerly sought. No class of workers here outrank women in opportunity, dignity, or the rewards that a sincere heart prizes most. To be sure, wealth cannot be won here, but a moderate income, sufficient for current needs, is certain to all faithful and efficient workers. A noisy fame is not to be attained, but a thousand homes will be your own and ten thousand hearts will bless and shelter you. Growth of brain, heart, and conscience is nowhere more certainly assured. There is no one-sided development, as in purely intellectual work, but thought and sympathy go hand-in-hand. It is a home-like place for a woman's soul to dwell in, this golden harvest-field of Christian work. The Ruths have been here long, as gleaners only. They have grown to be reapers at last. I might enumerate the societies for Home and Foreign Missions, Indian Reform, Associated Charities, and many other attractive lines of work, but my present object is to win your attention to the Woman's Christian Temperance Union as the most promising field of labor and reward that can be named for women, young or middle-aged or old. Let me tell you something of its history and aims:

The National Woman's Christian Temperance Union, with its thirty-eight auxiliary State and eight Territorial Unions, besides that of the District of Columbia, is the largest society ever composed exclusively of women, and conducted entirely by them. It is now organized in every State and Territory of the nation, except the Indian Territory, and locally in all important towns and cities. Great Britain, Canada, and Australia are also organized, and Mrs. Mary C. Leavitt, of Massachusetts, is making a preliminary reconnoissance for a World's Woman's Christian Temperance Union. As a general estimate (the returns being altogether incomplete), we think the number of local unions in the United States about ten thousand, with a membership of about one hundred and fifty thousand, besides numerous juvenile organizations. This society is the lineal descendant of the great Temperance Crusade of 1873-74, and is a union of Christian women of all churches, for the purpose of educating the young; forming a better public sentiment; reforming the drinking classes; transforming, by the power of divine grace, those who are enslaved by alcohol, and removing the dram-shop from our streets by law.

In the order of evolution, the departments of work are embraced under the following general classification: 1. Organizing; 2. Preventive; 3. Educational; 4. Evangelistic; 5. Social; 6. Legal.

Twelve years of constant study and experience have enabled us to reduce to a science the methods by which these departments have been made successful. These can be learned by active co-operation with the local society in your own town; by reading our weekly paper, *The Union Signal*, edited by Miss Mary Allen West, Chicago; "The Pathfinder" (our handbook), by Mrs. E. G. Greene, and by studying our national minutes and other practical helps, to be had by addressing Mrs. C. B. Buell, Headquarters National W. C. T. U., Chicago. For a history of the origin and growth of this great movement, and some knowledge of its leaders, I refer you to my own book, entitled "Woman and Temperance." (Same address.)

Hundreds of women have already become experts in this branch of social science and religious activity. As organizers, national, State, district, and county, they are kept constantly busy, and their income is provided by those for whom they labor. As local and State officers, salaries are often paid, but not as a rule, and in but one office of the national society. Nearly all these workers have learned to speak acceptably in public without manuscript or notes.

They are quiet, well-mannered, sensible women, who would compare favorably with the same number of teachers, artists, or musicians. Indeed, the majority of our leaders have, at some time, been teachers, but found the profession of Gospel temperance workers broader, just as independent, and no less beneficent. By the efforts of our societies the teaching of physiology and hygiene, with special reference to the effects of alcoholic stimulants and narcotics, has already been introduced by law into the public schools of seventeen States, and by the action of Congress into all the Territories and the District of Columbia. Kindergarten (with temperance adaptations) is one of our departments, also Kitchen Garden, both departments helping to prepare those who teach in them for the home cares which, later on, will come to most of our young workers. As corresponding secretaries of local unions, as private secretaries, clerks, and accountants, many are supporting themselves and helping the greatest of reforms; others, as organizers of Young Women's Christian Temperance Unions and Juvenile Societies. In our delightful " Flower Mission" there is great promise for willing hands, while our temperance, literature, and press departments offer the widest field for cultured brain and skilful pen. As lecturers in our departments of Heredity and Hygiene many a young lady physician has added to her power, while girls who would gladly have studied for the ministry have found a door wide open in our Gospel temperance meeting and credentials furnished by our department of evangelistic work.

Dear younger sisters, think about these things. They are " true, pure, lovely, and of good report." Talk them over in your Literary Society, your Chautauqua Literary and Scientific Circle, your quiet hour with loved ones at home. We want you, and perhaps you have need of us. Before long we shall establish a Training School with model Woman's Christian Temperance Union, model Juvenile Society, Kindergarten, Kitchen Garden, etc. If you should apply in sufficiently large numbers I am confident some wealthy temperance friend would help us to a "local habitation" for this use, but we have already begun with Summer Training Schools at several pleasant summer resorts. Lake Bluff is one of these, near Chicago, on the shore of Lake Michigan. Having been so many years a teacher, before enlisting in this grand Woman's Christian Temperance Union work, I have long meditated sending out this invitation to "sweet girl graduates" and any others to whom it might be like a friend's hand pointing to a safe and helpful avocation.

May our blessed Master guide you, and lead you wisely to decide the sacred question of your work "for God and Home and Native Land."

CHAPTER IV.

THE NEW IDEAL OF WOMANHOOD.

No doubt my readers have asked ere this the inevitable question: "Why does that seem natural and fitting for a young woman to do and to aspire to now which would have been no less improper than impossible a hundred years ago?" Sweet friends, it is because *the ideal of woman's place in the world is changing in the average mind.* For as the artist's ideal precedes his picture, so the ideal woman must be transformed before the actual one can be. In an age of brute force, the warrior galloping away to his adventures waved his mailed hand to the lady fair who was enclosed for safe keeping in a grim castle with moat and drawbridge. But to-day, when spirit force grows regnant, a woman can circumnavigate the globe alone, without danger of an uncivil word, much less of violence. We shall never span a wider chasm than this change implies. All our inventions have led up to it, and have in nothing else wrought out beneficence so great as they have accomplished here, purely by indirection. In brief, the barriers that have hedged women into one pathway and men into another, altogether different, are growing thin, as physical strength plays a less determining part in our life drama. All through the vegetable and animal kingdoms the fact of sex does not widely differentiate the broader fact of life, its environment and its pursuits. Hence, the immense separateness which sex is called in to explain when we reach the plane of humanity, is to be accounted for largely on artificial grounds. In Eden it did not exist, nor in the original plan of creation, as stated in these just and fatherly words: "And God said, 'Let us make man in our own image, after our own likeness. Let them have dominion.' . . . So God created man in His own image, in the image of God created he him, male and female created he them, and God blessed them, and said unto them, '. . . replenish the earth and subdue it . . . and have dominion over every living thing.'" After the fall came the curse, which may have been no part of the original design, and from which the Gospel's triumph is releasing us, for there is "neither male nor female in Christ Jesus." Who knows but that the origin of evil was contemporaneous with man's assertion of supremacy over one who was meant to be his equal comrade? If so, our Paradise regained will come only when the laureate's prophecy is realized :

> "Two heads in council, two beside the hearth,
> Two in the noisy business of the world,
> Two in the liberal offices of life ;
> Two plummets dropped to sound the abyss of science
> And the secrets of the mind."

The times when a new ideal is moulded, in Church, State, or society, mark the epochs of history. Amid what throes did Europe pass from that of supreme authority in the Church to the incomparably higher one of supreme liberty in conscience ; from the divine right of kings to the divine right of the people ! But there was to come a wider evolution of the same ideal—namely, the co-equal power of the co-partners, man and woman, in working out the problem of human destiny. This newest and noblest of ideals marks the transition from physical force ruling to spiritual force recognized. The gradual adjustment of every-day occupation, custom and law, to this new ideal, marks ours as a transition period. Those who have the most enlargement of opportunity to hope for from the change, will, in the nature of the case, move on most rapidly into the new conditions, and this helps to explain, I think, why women seem to be climbing more rapidly than men, to-day, the heights of spiritual power, with souls more open to the "skyey influences" of the oncoming age.

More women study to-day than men; a greater proportion travel abroad for purposes of culture; a larger share are moral and religious. Half of the world's wisdom, more than half its purity, and nearly all its gentleness, are to-day to be set down on woman's credit side. Weighted with the alcohol and tobacco habits, Brother Jonathan will have to make better time than he is doing now, if he keeps step with Sister Deborah across the threshold of the twentieth century. For the law of survival of the fittest will inevitably choose that member of the firm who is cleanliest, most wholesome, most accordant with God's laws of nature and of grace, to survive. To the blindness or fatuity which renders him oblivious of the fact that the coming woman is already well-nigh here, our current writer of the W. D. Howells and Henry James school owes the dreary monotony of his "society novel." Not more "conventional" was the style of art known as "Byzantine," which repeated with barren iteration its placid and colorless "type," than are the pages of this dreary pair, whose books will put a period to the literary sentence of their age. The "American novel" will not be written until the American woman, a type now to be found in Michigan, Boston, Cornell, and other universities, shall have taken her place, twentieth-century product that she is, beside the best survivals of young men in similar institutions, and wrought out the Home, the Church, the State that are to be. Measuring each other on all planes, these life partners will know each other's value, and no appeal to the divorce court will be made to relieve them, a few years after marriage, from an incompatibility that has ripened into open war. Happy homes will dot the country from shore to shore, in which both the man and the woman will do their best to lift the world toward God.

"Self-knowledge, self-reverence, and self-control: these three alone lead life to sovereign power," and these are fast becoming essential to any ideal of womanly character which the modern age will recognize as the product of its institutions. Of self-knowledge, these talks have said much. Self-reverence I would fain help you to develop in your character as a woman. If my dear mother did me one crowning kindness it was in making me believe that next to being an angel, the greatest bestowment of God is to make one a woman. With what contempt she referred to the old Jewish formula in which the less refined sex rolled out the words, "I thank Thee, O God, that Thou hast not made me a woman," and with what pathos she repeated the gentle prayer of the other, "I thank Thee, O God, that Thou hast made me as it pleased Thee," with the pithy comment, "What could have pleased Him better, I should like to know, than to make one so rare, so choice, so spirit-nal as woman is?" Perhaps some of you may have thought you wanted to be a boy, but I seriously doubt it. You may have wanted a boy's freedom, his independence, his healthful, unimpeding style of dress, but I do not believe any true girl could ever have been coaxed to be a boy. Reverence yourself, then, if you would learn one of the first elements of "How to Win" in this great world race, with its "go-as-you-please" terms, but its relentless penalties for failure.

What will the new ideal of woman *not* be? Well, for example, she will never be written down in the hotel register by her husband after this fashion: "John Smith and Wife." He would as soon think of her writing "Mrs. John Smith and Husband." Why does it not occur to any one to designate him thus? Simply because he is so much more than that. He is a leading force in the affairs of the Church; he helps decide who shall be pastor. (So will she.) He is, perhaps, the village physician, or merchant (so she will be, perhaps—indeed, they are oftentimes in partnership, nowadays, and I have found their home a blessed one.) He is the village editor. (Very likely she will be associate.) He is a voter. (She will be, beyond a peradventure.) For the same reason you will never read of her marriage that "the minister pronounced them MAN and *wife*," for that functionary would have been just as likely to pronounce them "husband and woman," a form of expression into which the regulation reporter will be likely to fall one of these days, it being, really, not one whit more idiotic than the time-worn phrase, "man and wife." The ideal woman of the future will never be designated as "the *Widow* Jones," because she will be so much more than that

—"a provider" for her children, "a power" in the Church, "a felt force" in the State. I think George Eliot is the first woman to attain the post-mortem honor of having her husband called "her widower," John W. Cross having been thus indicated in English papers of the period. A turn about is fair play, and the phrase is really quite refreshing to one's sense of justice. The ideal woman will not write upon her visiting-card, nor insist on having her letters addressed, to Mrs. John Smith, or Mrs. General Smith, as the case may be, but if her maiden name were Jones, she will fling her banner to the breeze as " Mrs. Mary Jones-Smith," and will be sure to make it honorable. She will not be the lay figure made and provided to illustrate the fashions of Monsieur Worth and lesser lights of the same guild, but will insist that the goddess Hygeia is the only true modiste, and will dutifully obey her orders. As the Louvre Gallery proves that when men were but the parasites of the court they, too, decked themselves with earrings, high heels, powdered hair and gaudy garments, so the distorted figures in the detestable fashion-plates of today are the irrefutable proofs of woman's fractional estate; but this will not be so to-morrow, when she finds her kingdom—which is her own true self. The ideal woman will cease to heed the cruel " Thus far and no farther," which has issued from the pinched lips of old Dame Custom, checking her ardent steps throughout all the ages past, and will be studious only to hear the kindly " Thus far and no farther" of God.

The ideal woman will play Beatrice to man's Dante in the Inferno of his passions. She will give him the clew out of materialism's Labyrinth. She will be civilization's

Una, taming the Lion of disease and misery. The State shall no longer go limping on one foot through the years, but shall march off with steps firm and equipoised. The keen eye and deft hand of the housekeeper shall help to make its every-day walks wholesome; the skill in detail, trustworthiness in finance, motherliness in sympathy, so long extolled in private life, shall exalt public station. Indeed, if I were asked the mission of the ideal woman, I would reply: IT IS TO MAKE THE WHOLE WORLD HOMELIKE. Some one has said that "Temperament is the climate of the individual," but home is woman's climate, her vital breath, her native air. A true woman carries home with her everywhere. Its atmosphere surrounds her; its mirror is her face; its music attunes her gentle voice; its longitude may be reckoned from wherever you happen to find her. But "home's not merely four square walls."

Some people once thought it was, and they thought, also, that you might as well throw down its Lares and Penates as to carry away its weaving-loom and spinning-wheel. But it survived this spoliation; and when women ceased to pick their own geese and do their own dyeing, it still serenely smiled. The sewing-machine took away much of its occupation; the French and Chinese laundries have intruded upon its domain; indeed the next generation will no doubt turn the cook-stove out of doors, and the housekeeper, standing at the telephone, will order better cooked meals than almost any one has nowadays, sent from scientific caterers by pneumatic tubes, and the débris thereof returned to a general cleaning-up establishment; while houses will be heated, as they are now lighted and supplied with water, from general reservoirs.

Women are fortunate in belonging to the less tainted half of the race. Dr. Benjamin Ward Richardson tells us that but for this conserving fact it would deteriorate to the point of failure. A bright old lady said, after viewing a brewery, distillery, and tobacco factory : " A'n't I thankful that the women folks hain't got all that stuff to chew and smoke and swallow down !" It behooves us to offset force of muscle by force of heart, that what our strong brothers have done to subdue the material world for us, who are not their equals in physical strength, may be offset by what we shall achieve for them in bringing in the reign of "Sweeter manners, purer laws." For the world is slowly making the immense discovery that not what woman *does*, but what she *is*, makes home a possible creation. It is the Lord's ark, and does not need steadying ; it will survive the wreck of systems and the crash of theories, for the home is but the efflorescence of woman's nature under the nurture of Christ's Gospel. She came into the college and elevated it, into literature and hallowed it, into the business world and ennobled it. She will come into government and purify it, into politics and cleanse its Stygian pool, for woman will make homelike every place she enters, and she will enter every place on this round earth. Any custom, or traffic, or party on which a woman cannot look with favor is irrevocably doomed. Its welcome of her presence and her power is to be the final test of its fitness to survive. All gospel civilization is radiant with the demonstration of this truth : " It is not good for man to be alone." The most vivid object lesson on history's page is the fact that his deterioration is in exact proportion to his isolation from the home of woman's pure companionship. To my own grateful thought, the most sacred significance of woman's philanthropic work to-day lies in the fact that she occupies the outer circle in this tremendous evolution of the Christian idea of home. Ours is a high and sacred calling. Out of pure hearts fervently, let us love God and humanity; so shall we be Christ's disciples, and so shall we safely follow on to know the work whereunto we have been called. "'Tis home where'er the heart is," and no true mother, sister, daughter, or wife can fail to go in spirit after her beloved and tempted ones, as their adventurous steps enter the labyrinth of the world's temptations. We cannot call them back. "All before them lies the way."

There is but one remedy : we must bring the home to them, for they will not return to it. Still must their mothers walk beside them, sweet and serious, and clad in the garments of power. The occupations, pleasures, and ambitions of men and women must not diverge so widely from each other. Potent beyond all other facts of every-day experience is the rapidly increasing similarity between the pursuits of these two fractions that make up the human integer. When brute force reigned, this *rapport* was at zero. "Impedimenta to the rear," was the command of Cæsar and the rule of every warrior—women and children being the hindrances referred to. But to-day there is not a motto more popular than that of the inspired old German, "Come, let us live for our children ;" and as for women, "the world is all before them where to choose."

No greater good can come to the manhood of the world than is prophesied in the increasing community of thought and works between it and the world's womanhood. The growing individuality, independence and prestige of the gentler sex steadily require from the stronger a higher standard of character and purer habits of life. This blessed consummation, so devoutly to be wished, is hastened, dear girlish hearts, by every prayer you offer, by every hymn you sing, by every loving errand of your willing feet and gentle hands. You are the true friends of tempted manhood, bewildered youth, and every little child. The steadfast faith and loyal, patient work you are to do, in the white fields of reform, will be the mightiest factor in woman's contribution to the solution of this Republic's greatest problem, and will have their final significance in the thought and purpose, not that the world shall come into the home, but that the home, embodied and impersonated in its womanhood, shall go forth into the world.

I have no fears for the women of America. They will never content themselves remaining stationary in methods or in policy, much less sound a retreat in their splendid warfare against the saloon in law and in politics. The tides of the mother's heart do not change; we can count upon them always. The voice of Miriam still cheers the brave advance, and all along the line we hear the battle-cry: "Speak unto the children of Israel, that they go forward."

CHAPTER V.

THE NEW IDEAL OF MANHOOD.

LET us remember, then, that the Ideal of Womanhood, as it exists in the minds of the grandest-natured men, is changing rapidly. But as you study "How to Win," conforming your plan of life to the new ideal which you must clearly see "in your mind's eye, Horatio," before you can proceed to study, much less to win, a certain shy question is sure to haunt your brain. "Uttered or unexpressed," it will be there, and it will be this: "Elder sister, coming freshly from life's battlefield where banners wave and squadrons wheel, you tell us that the ideal of woman is gradually changing; *but how is it with the Ideal of Man?*" Ah, gentle hearts, you do well to ask that question; it is "part of the price;" not to propound it, either in the silence of your own heart or the half-apologetic tone with which I grew familiar in my teaching days (when girlish confidences were reposed in me so often), would be confessing judgment as not downright womanly yourselves. Yes, the ideal of man is changing—as it must—to keep pace with its blessed correlate. The ideal man is a "Brother of Girls," as the choice Arab proverb phrases it. He is chivalric, but the chivalry of justice outranks that of manner and romance upon his Bill of Rights. He never says, because he never thinks, "you are only a girl," for he has grown to be the antithesis of the Jew who thanked God who had not made him a woman, and honestly believes that she is "the crowning work of God." He values her esteem and love as the most priceless of all benedictions this side of heaven, and to make himself worthy of them he sedulously determines to be free from every habit which would be unworthy of or distasteful to her. He recognizes himself as her comrade, not her master, and rejoices in their joint-partnership in all this world affords. He asserts over her no rights whatever, but is a man so good and noble that his happiness is her law, even as hers is his delight. He would deem it beneath his dignity to lay commands upon his equal, and would be as much ashamed to hint at woman's subjection, as some crude, old-time men and all barbarous nations are proud to assert it. Whatever property he may have or accumulate, he regards as one half hers, not of grace but of debt, and anticipates, by his own action, those laws which will erelong assert this equitable claim. He does not think that woman exists primarily for him or for the home, but as a daughter of God, whose duties are, first of all, to her own nature and to Him by whom that nature was endowed. Similarity, not differentiation, of surroundings and pursuits is what he seeks, perceiving this to be great nature's law in all the lower forms of mated life, and believing the departure from this rule in human history to have been a temporary concession to the age of brute force. He does not ask the narrow question, "Is she good enough for certain professions, avocations, and spheres?" but rather, "Are they good enough for her?" and this he leaves for her to settle, perceiving that "under grace" she may very properly inquire, "Who made thee a judge or a rewarder over me?" These are some of the traits of that great, high-souled, generous nature, that "Mother's boy" who is to be. Enough specimens have strayed into this century to show us his outline, and make us sure that "the coming man" is not far off. Womanhood, in the new age, shall rejoice in this companionship, and thousands, bravely living now their true and individual life alone, loyal to this ideal, shall find him in the world unseen, and, like Endymion to Diana, in Longfellow's sweet words:

> "Shall whisper, in their song,
> Where hast *thou* staid so long?"

Some glimpse of this ideal came to me at sixteen years of age, in the grief of the most sorrowful experience my life had known up to that hour. I had a brother who met my views of what a youth should be. He treated me as his playmate, his brave, adventurous comrade. We read the same books; shared the same country sports and rambles; looked out upon life with aims and purposes almost identical; and talked of "all the wonder that should be." To speak and write was his most cherished dream, as it was mine. On the Fourth of July in our rural neighborhood, we had our little celebrations, and he used to say to me: "Wouldn't you like to carry the flag part of the time?" Whereupon I was not the least bit backward about coming forward to indulge in this proud and patriotic exercise. To be sure, our flag was only a pillow-case with red calico stripes sewed on, gilt paper stars pinned in the corner, and a broomstick for the flag-staff (prophetic emblem!), but it was the insignia of that kindly mother named "America," who was so good and helpful to all her boys and girls.

THE NEW IDEAL OF MANHOOD.   61

Sometimes he made the "Fourth of July speech," and sometimes I did, and our voices sounded most harmonious as we led our playmates in the song of songs,

> "Forever float that standard sheet;
> Where breathes the foe but falls before us,
> With freedom's soil beneath our feet
> And freedom's banner streaming o'er us!"

You see this was lovely to contemplate, and a clear case of "We, Us, and Company" all the way through.

But that boy grew right on, and came at last to be "of age;" soon after which mystical epoch, "Election Day" arrived, which was thought to be a sacred time at our house, and he went to deposit his first ballot. I never understood why our paths should thus diverge, so relentlessly and so suddenly for all time. Father and mother had trained us both "for God and Home and Native Land." They had built their life, their character, and teaching into us steadily through the quiet, earnest years. I felt, girl as I was, that the loss was not a small one to the country I loved, when she lost my vote. The Republic profited but half, when it might have registered the full force of our home teaching; it needed mother and all "the women folks" to offset the self-indulgent vote that sheltered the liquor traffic and other crimes under the ægis of law. There flushed upon me then, as I watched the brother I loved, a vision of what he might become, could his "Mother and the Girls" go with him into his life pursuits. I saw, with all the vividness of truth, the ideal which, across the wide spaces of the years, I have tried to picture in these pages, and I want you to believe in, and to cherish the same. Sojourner

Truth says, "I live on my ideas," the amended version of which human-like utterance is, "I live by my Ideals." We all do this, and, under the great question "How to Win," comes the greater one, "For what sake do I care to win at all ?" Surely for what, except to attain more nearly to the heights where God's ideals of woman's character and its immortal correlate dwell in the light of a future and a better world. Not of the "Woman Question" have I been writing in this chapter on "Ideals;" but of the deeper, broader, and more sacred *Human* Question, for the two halves of humanity must rise or fall together, "dwarfed or Godlike, bond or free." Poetry proves this no more than plainest prose. Take the late figures about woman's higher education, given by Hon. Carroll D. Wright, of Boston, Chief of the Bureau of Statistics. Of seven hundred and five graduates who returned replies to his questions, their average age being twenty-eight years, five hundred and nine were living in single-blessedness, against one hundred and ninety-six who had been married an average of six years. The Chicago *Tribune*, commenting upon these facts, says :

"It might be ungraciously said that their higher education had led them to fix a higher value on their marriage values, but we do not believe that the secret lies in the enhancing of values. It might be said again that young men have a secret fear of educated young women, when it comes to taking them as partners for life, and are apt to regard them much as Dr. Holmes does his college young lady, Lurida, ' the female terror.' The cause, however, lies still deeper, we fancy. The average of women, owing to the scarcity of appropriate labor on the one hand, and their inability to perform profitable labor on the other, marry to be taken care of. The thoroughly educated young woman discovers that she can earn a good living, and consequently it is not necessary for her to marry in order to be supported. Being able to support herself, she is in a position to wait until her real complement comes along, and not

THE NEW IDEAL OF MANHOOD. 63

take chances in the marriage lottery. In other words, knowledge is power to her. In this respect as well as in all others, the logical inference from the report is that the higher education of women is conducive to their health, happiness, and usefulness."

Now, as an orthodox friend of the Human Race, in both its fractions, Man and Woman, I am not more glad of the fact stated in this editorial comment because of the good it brings to young ladies, than because of the good it prophesies for young gentlemen. I have long believed that when the question of a life-companionship shall be decided on its merits, pure and simple, and not complicated with the other questions, " Did she get a good home ?" " Is he a good provider ?" " Will she have plenty of money ?"; then will come the first fair chance ever enjoyed by young manhood for the building up of genuine character and conduct. For it is an immense temptation to the " sowing of wild oats," when the average youth knows that the smiles he covets most will be his all the same, no matter whether he smokes, swears, drinks beer, and plays cards or not. The knowledge, on his part, that the girls in his village and " set " have no way out of dependence, reproach, and oddity, except to say " Yes" when he chooses to " propose ;" that they dare not frown on his lower mode of life ; that the world is all before him where to *choose ;* that not one girl in one hundred has been endowed with the talent and the pluck that make her independent of him and his ilk ; all this gives him a sense of freedom to do wrong which, added to inherited appetite and outward temptation, is impelling the youth of our day to ruin with a force strong as gravitation, and relentless as fate. Then, the utterly false sense of his own value and importance which " Young

America" acquires, from seeing the sweetest, truest, most attractive beings on earth thus virtually subject to him, often develops a lordliness of manner which is too pitiful for words, in boys who, otherwise, would have been modest, sensible, and brotherly young fellows, such as we are, most of all, likely to find in co-education schools, where girls take their full share of the prizes, and many of them have in mind "a career." A thousand forces in law and gospel are to-day conspiring for the deliverance of our young men from the snares of their present artificial environment and estimate of their own value; but the elevation of their sisters to the plane of perfect financial independence, from which they can dictate the equitable terms, "You must be as pure and true as you require me to be, ere I give you my hand," is the brightest hope that gleams in the sky of modern civilization for our brothers; and the greater freedom of women to make of marriage an affair of the heart and not of the purse, is the supreme result of Christianity up to this hour.

It has seemed good and proper to me, thus at the outset, to put before you some general notion of my theories of life, that, coming down to the picture's "filling in," you might more justly estimate the relation of the parts to the whole. Earlier in life, I might not have dealt thus frankly, but at its serene meridian, blessed by the kind relationship of "Aunt" to a lovely niece already in her twentieth year, I can afford to speak to you, my wide-awake readers, with the freedom permitted by advancing years and dignities! For the rest of this series, let me be more specific as to the methods by which I have seen girls win character, knowledge, reputation, and success. By this I do not mean their winning on the world's public stage, where so few figures find room—only a thousand famous people being there now, of all the thousand million that exist. For, though the printing-press and swift means of conveying one's self and one's thought tend toward a vastly and constantly increasing democracy of fame, I am to talk, in these confidential pages, of private rather than of public life. "Act *well* your part, there all the honor lies," and in all likelihood if you but know what your part is, and do not by mistake get that belonging to somebody else, you will so thoroughly enjoy it that you will act it well, and life, here and hereafter, shall be to you "one grand, sweet song."

CHAPTER VI.

THE BEAUTIFUL.

WITHOUT beauty it is impossible to win. It has been well and wisely said :

> "The beautiful are never desolate,
> But some one always loves them."

The truth of this saying early forced itself on my attention and put a minor strain into the sweet psalm of my youthful life. The plain-faced girl who has a pretty sister commands my inmost sympathy; for just there I have been, and in a soul most sensitive and timid have hidden away the pathos of that evermore difficult and unspoken situation. To have beside you, nearer than any other human being, a sister, fair and winsome, whose ribbons always "match," whose hair takes kindly to the latest style, whose gloves invariably fit, and whose bonnet cannot be unbecoming; to know yourself for a creature awkward and unadorned, upon whom this gracious, loving comrade at your side vainly expends all the skill of fingers deft and delicate—this is not what a girl's heart would choose. To hear the door-bell ring at evening, and see from upper windows the freshly-garnished young collegian enter, asking for "Miss Mary;" to be counted out so often, when she is counted in, and to know that the rounding of a few facial angles, the brightening of a glance, the deepening of color on a cheek, would have made one's outlook on the great, fascinating world so much more lovely—this is to give to a girl's heart "thoughts that do often lie too deep for tears."

I can look back now, across the infinite spaces of thirty thoughtful years, and be touched with tenderest pity for that crude self, so long since dead, to whom all this was so real and oftentimes so painful. In the long and quiet interval I have mused much why these things were, and I have set it down as a principle that only the beautiful are loved, or ought to be, since only they fall in with the plan of our beautiful God, and of this transcendently glorious universe which is the profile view of that Face whose radiance shall flood our immortality. But the "ripe, round, mellow years" have lifted the mists of my life's morning, and given me glimpses of that open secret, most ineffable and blessed, *How to Be Beautiful*. It is not in paints and powders, not in ruffles, ribbons, or false ringlets, and not in the use of "Pears' Soap" or the "Balm of a Thousand Flowers." For one learns, after a while, that this face and form we wear about are but a mask, a thin, almost transparent veil, through which the spirit looks, coyly at first, but later on, with calm and steady gaze. Every seven years the veil must be renewed; with time come wrinkles, where the soul breaks through, and our whole history is written in them for those who have learned to read. What is behind this changeful face, moulding and making it forever new? It is one's own true self. Nay, more, the face itself is as clay in the hands of the potter to the spirit that lies back of it. There are scientists who teach that it is possible to modify the outline of an eyebrow, the bulge of a forehead, the protuberances of a cranium, by the slow processes of an education which shall develop memory at the expense of perception, or conventionality at the expense of reason. There are others who declare that every person's outward seeming rightly studied, the angles of his jaw and forehead, the direction of ear and nostril, the contour of lips and chin, are a perfect self-revealment to the specialist in physiognomy. For myself, I believe the day is not distant when the schools shall teach these principles, and in that day the physical basis of character, the expression given by outward form to inward grace or gracelessness, how to overcome the one and cultivate the other, shall replace much of what the schoolmen of our time are serving up under the name of "Knowledge." I believe the day is not far off when the symbolism of human features shall be so based on scientific research, that a rogue can by no means palm himself off as a saint, and the wolf in sheep's clothing will be a physical impossibility. We write our own hieroglyphics on our own faces as plainly as ever etchings are traced by artists. Perfect unity with God's laws written in our members, obedience to the decalogue of natural law, and the ritual of this body which was meant to be the temple of the Holy Ghost, would have made us all beautiful to start with ; would have endowed us by inheritance with the fascinating graces of Hebe and Apollo. But generations of pinched waists and feet, of the cerebellum overheated by its wad of hair, the vital organs cramped, the free step impeded, and the gracious human form bandaged and dwarfed, all these exact from every new-born child the penalty of law inexorable, law outraged and trampled under foot through long and painful years. When I note the mincing gait of fashionable girlhood, the betwisted ringlets, compressed waist, and overlying draperies; when I contemplate the fact that the edicts of the theatre and the demi-monde, from which come the "latest styles," have deprived us of watch-pockets and burdened us with "bustles," I am more nearly disheartened about women than anything else can make me. Like an irate physician of New York, "I wish, since those wasp-waists are so nearly asunder, I had a pair of scissors that the work might be completed." A heathen woman in China on seeing one of our abominable current fashion plates, exclaimed : " You say we do wrong to bind up the foot, but you Christians kill God's life when you bind up a woman's waist." The graveyards are full of victims of diseases that came of tight-lacing, and the hospitals groan with their degenerate offspring; while the puny physique and delicate health of American women is a reproach among the nations; but I have yet to see a single one of our species who will admit that her corset is "the least bit tight," and no one seems to perceive that this claim proves her to be a downright monstrosity in form, since the ample and stately Venus of Milo is an acknowledged standard. But when women, now old, tell me of the brass stomachers and terrific high heels worn by their grandmothers, and that in their own youth they "strung their corsets" by making a fulcrum of the bed-post, and pulling with all their might and main, I "breathe freer," metaphorically speaking, think that some women, at least, are coming to their senses, and keep urging the introduction of hygiene as a special study in all branches of the public schools. We need this as women hardly less than do our brothers, for I verily believe, and shamefacedly confess, that the corset-habit among women is as difficult to break as the alcohol and tobacco habit among men. If the laws of God that seek the health of the body were obeyed but by a single generation, the next one would be physically beautiful. I am always glad when one of our "society girls" says to me, "Coffee and tea hurt my complexion, so I have left off drinking them ;" or, "Greasy food coarsens one's looks and I can't afford to eat it ;" or, "Buckwheat cakes and sausage make my face 'break out,' so, though I love them dearly (!) they have been put aside." The motive might be higher. It should be grounded in a reverent purpose to know and do the will of God at the table where grace is so often said over most graceless food, but untold good will come of a simpler and more wholesome diet, no matter what is its procuring cause. The desire to be beautiful is instinctive, because we were all meant to be so and may all claim our heritage upon this spiritual plane, even though so ruthlessly defrauded of it, on the material plane, by the ignorant excesses of our ancestors and the follies of our own untaught years. But while I would beg my clear-headed American girls to make a special study of the sacred laws of health, I would still more urgently impress the importance of the spiritual law of beauty upon their sensitive young hearts. It is not left to a fish to determine whether its mouth shall draw up or down, but that matter *is* left to a human being's choice. A chimpanzee has no control over his wrinkles, but a man and woman have. A dog has his hair cut in ways to suit purchasers, and a boy at the present day makes himself a spectacle to the human race, by the "penitentiary clip," but a young lady can greatly modify and improve her *tout ensemble* by the style of her coiffure. She can refrain from piercing her ears, bangling her arms, *à la* Piute Indian belle; emulating the heels of a French ballet dancer; deforming her waist; "banging" her hair; or sporting an aviary upon her hat. The most shocking experience of my life this year was consequent upon an unwary visit to a Boston milliner's establishment, where without stopping to say, "By your leave," an attendant perched upon my head a fifteen-dollar bonnet crowned with five canaries! I asked them where they got the brilliant birds of which their show-cases were full, being curious to know if they were slaughtered by the Zulus of Africa or the wild Islanders of Terra del Fuego; whereupon they intimated that there had been great sparrow-killing in America this year and that the feathers of these little creatures had been dyed. This helped to explain the new style and the superabundance of material. If Indians in Alaska should so trick themselves out, as an offset to that leaden sky, one might better comprehend the motive, but for Christian Americans to go to church wearing a small flock of birdlings and piously listen to the sweet lesson, "One of them shall not fall to the ground without your Father," is a curiosity of cruelty for which no adequate explanation can by any possibility be furnished. Now, aside from all that I have said about the insanity of fashion, about hygiene and outward adorning, about the possibility of modifying both "bumps" and features, let me emphasize the highest method of acquiring that beauty which is the result of one's own inner life. Behind everything there is a thought. As a man thinketh so is he. Expression is the loftiest and the final charm in every human face. While it is right, indeed a heavenly intuition, to desire beauty, and while attention to the laws of hygiene, good taste, and good behavior mightily conduce to it, heavenly thoughts are the only sure recipe for a countenance of heavenly expression. St. Cecilia heard the music of the upper courts, and hence her face mirrors its ethereal loveliness. It is not only true that prayer will cause a man to cease from sinning, even as sin will cause a man to cease from prayer; but it is also true that no heart can be lifted up toward God as a lily lifts its chalice to the sun, without the face beaming with a light which never shone or sea or shore, but which reflects the shekinah of the upper sanctuary. The ever-welcome, ugly face of a beautiful soul is vastly more endearing and endeared to wistful human eyes than the classic brow of Eugenie, the sparkling eyes of Patti, or the statuesque pose of Mary Anderson. Their beauty is on the material plane, and evanescent, but this is on the spiritual plane, and beauty of expression shall endure and grow forever if we but keep on thinking thoughts of peace, purity, and tenderness.

Be true to the dream of your youth. Hold fast to the highest ideals that flash upon your vision in hours of exaltation. But no guest can ever keep you company, so rare and radiant as the Holy Guest (miscalled a "Ghost" in theological nomenclature), and He comes to us as the present Christ, the only antecedent of a present Heaven.

None but the beautiful can win, since beauty is the normal condition of us all, and whatever is abnormal is in so far a failure. But God is good. His tender mercies are over all His works; He makes it possible for every human being to be beautiful, and the method of becoming so involves the serene and steady search after the highest happiness.

But let us not forget that while this law of physical beauty holds in full force, its application is no less exact when we emerge upon the broader consideration of our theme. For there are so many kinds of beauty after which one may strive that we are bewildered by the bare attempt to number them. There is beauty of manner, of utterance, of achievement, of reputation, of character, any one of which outweighs beauty of person, even in the scales of society, to say nothing of celestial values. Cultivate most of the kind that lasts longest. The beautiful face with nothing back of it lacks the "staying qualities" that are necessary to those who would be winners in the race of life. It is not the first mile-post but the last that tells the story ; not the outward bound steed but the one on the "home stretch" that we note as victor. The loom of life turns out many different fabrics. Is the beauty that you seek the gossamer of a day or the royal purple of a century ? Beauty of manner, tender considerateness, reverence, and equipoise will make it impossible for you ever to be desolate, and will insure your always being loved. No physical defect, however irremediable, bars you from this choicest of all exterior attractions. Beauty of utterance has a fadeless charm ; opens all hearts whose key it is worth while to wish for ; and makes those once obscure, the favorites of fortune, the heroes of society, the peers of kings. Burns was a Highland peasant, but the magic of his song made him the idol of a nation, and winsomeness of speech will always win, whether upon the world's great stage or in the sheltered home life. Beauty of achievement, whether in overcoming a hasty temper, or a habit of exaggeration; in exploring a Continent with Stanley, or guiding well the ship of state with Gladstone, is always fascinating, and whether known in a circle large as the equator or only in the family circle at home, those who are in this fashion beautiful are never desolate and some one always loves them. Beauty of reputation is a mantle of spotless ermine in which if you are but enwrapped you shall receive the homage of those about you, as real, as ready, and as spontaneous as any ever paid to personal beauty in its most entrancing hour. Some sort of reputation you must have, whether you will or no. In school, in church, at home, and in society you carry ever with you the wings of a good or the ball and chain of a bad reputation. Resolve to make it beautiful, clear, shining, gracious. This is within your power though the color of your eyes and hair is not. But reputation, after all, is but the shadow cast by character; and beauty, in this best and highest sense, commands all forces worth the having, in all worlds. Every form of attractiveness confesses the primacy of this. Beauty of character includes every good of which a human heart can know, and makes the woman who possesses it a princess in Israel, whose home is everybody's heart, and whose heaven is everywhere. The dullest eyes may reflect this beauty; the palest cheek bloom with it; the most unclassic lips may be enwreathed with its smile of ineffable good-will and heavenly joy. For beauty of character comes only from loving obedience to every known law of God in nature and in grace. Lovingly to learn and dutifully to obey these laws of our beneficent Father is to live. Anything less is but to vegetate. Dear younger sisters, " let us keep our Heavenly Father in the midst," let us be beautiful, for we were meant to be ; let us not only desire but determine to be *winners*, but most of all let us remember with each tick of the brain in a thought, and of faith in a prayer, that "*the King's daughter must be all glorious* WITHIN."

CHAPTER VII.

THE DECALOGUE OF NATURAL LAW.

WHEN travelling South for temperance purposes in 1881, I met Mrs. Jefferson Davis in Memphis, Tenn. My accomplished hostess, Mrs. J. C. Johnson, was at that time President of the Women's Christian Association, of which Mrs. Davis was Secretary, and so the interview came about most naturally. Of all the gifted women it has been my good fortune to know, Mrs. Davis was chief in the rare and radiant grace of conversation. Everything she said that morning was worthy to be written down, but the sentence that returns to me most frequently was this, "*Simply to breathe is joy enough for a well-bred English girl.*" Of superb physique herself, Mrs. Davis had been contrasting the customs of the two countries in respect to out-door exercise, to the disadvantage of American women when compared with our robust British cousins. Often in heated car and stifling audience-room have I bemoaned the lot that made pure air to me an almost unknown blessing, and wistfully repeated those reviving words, "simply to breathe is joy enough for a well-bred English girl." It is at least a consolation to know that we long for better things, that something in us reaches out after them, for as a German poet writes, "Whatever we greatly admire and profoundly desire to become, that we in some measure already are."

Born for the big, blessed, inspiring "Outdoors," we women shall never rest until we rejoice once more in our paradise regained. I wonder if this is not a secret wish in every woman's soul. It astonished and amused me not a little, though there was really untold pathos in it, when a bright young friend of mine responded to my question, "What do you think I should really enjoy most of anything on earth?" with the unheard-of statement, "Well, in spite of your demure ways and devotion to philanthropy, I really believe you'd like best of all to put on a gymnastic suit and climb a tree!"

The breezy, out-door life has an inextinguishable charm for all women with whom I have exchanged confidences on the subject, but the impeding costume and the conventionalities of society have checked their development, and given them over to furnace-air, flabby muscle, and sluggish circulation. Unfortunately, the magazines for children and young people accept the situation as they find it instead of trying to create a better one; descant on "Sports for Boys," who are sure to disport themselves extensively without suggestion, and are silent about "Exercise for Girls." Mothers give a whip and a sled to their sons (whose innate sense of control needs no abetting, and who have the freedom of all out-doors without so much as saying "by your leave"), and a doll and set of dishes to their girls, whose maternal instincts are sufficiently God-implanted to need no special forcing, and who will "keep house," all their lives long anyhow, and with a steadiness that cannot fail to make them fractional women, physically at least. A more philosophical view of education by toys (the old-fashioned home-kindergarten whose influence doubtless reaches farther than we think), instead of intensifying unduly traits already inherent, would change the playthings squarely about, thus developing more strongly the fatherly nature of one and evolving the courage and physical strength of the other. I sincerely hope that Chautauqua University, which has given us almost everything else under the sun, will establish a gymnasium and promulgate a series of lessons on "All men (and women) their own athletes." Please take notice that in that happy case I wish to be enrolled as the earliest applicant for "training!" Let us also have the tricycle domesticated as well as the saddle-horse, bow and arrow, and lawn tennis. Speaking of the last delightful game, whose inventor ought to be canonized by womenkind, reminds me of what our girls ruefully declare with many a deprecating glance at wardrobes to be mended: "It takes half the fun out of this game when we stumble over our skirts." And one who watches them might add commiseratingly, "Yes, and when you are betrayed by your high heels, well-nigh smothered by your tight waists, or blinded by the sun from which no friendly hat-brim shields you."

But let us make devout acknowledgment that the splendid march of science is slowly "moving on the enemy's works" and the tyranny of fashion is not so unquestioned or complete as it was even ten years ago. Within a week a friend sent me the New York *Cloak and Ladies' Wear Review*, wherein my eyes were gladdened by a "Department of Dress Reform" in which, alongside of monstrosities in the "Fashion Plates" that made my cheeks tingle with shame, were the calm, womanly utterances of those who have studied this most vital theme from a practical and scientific point of view, and the promise of more to follow in future issues of the magazine, for which I wish sensible women would subscribe. Some recent "inside views" relating to the origin of fashions are in place just here, from a trustworthy New York authority:

"'Don't try to reason logically about fashion,' said a dainty little milliner, shaking her head disconsolately, as she reviewed the latest pattern plates, and frowned as they failed to meet with her approval; 'for of all illogical and unreasonable laws those which govern fashion are positively the worst. Perhaps you imagine that the various styles which invade the ladies of to-day are the result of carefully considered experiments, or that meetings are held and certain fashions unanimously declared desirable. You make a great mistake. Such is not the case. Nearly all the fashions which have become popular in civilized countries have simply been the result of accident. I am not exaggerating. Let me give you illustrations. In France, the beautiful Ferronière was once—I grieve to say it—smoking a cigarette. She was not accustomed to indulge in that habit, you may be surprised to hear, and met with a slight accident. She removed the cigarette from her mouth, held it between her fingers, forgot, presumably, that it was there, was about to rest her forehead on her hand, when the lighted end of the cigarette came in contact with her brow and burned it. It made an ugly scar. Do you think that worried her? Not a bit of it. The next day she covered the scar with a jewel, and the following week every lady of the court, who valued her reputation as a society star, wore a similar jewel on her forehead. Ha! ha! That's one instance. The Princess of Wales, as everybody

knows, has an unfortunate limp, which nothing under the
sun could render beautiful. But the foolish London ladies
seeing this said to themselves: "Dear me! how *chic* that
limp is." The "Alexandra limp," as it was called, became extremely fashionable, and it was obtained by making
the heel of one boot shorter than that of the other. The
Princess of Wales has also a very long and meagre neck.
She was absolutely obliged to wear only high dresses, close
up to the throat. But the thousands of English ladies who
had not very long necks followed her example, and made
themselves ridiculous. Dear me! How stupid the fashionable world is!'

"The little milliner sighed at the frailties of her sex,
but tortured herself by relating still more of them. 'Do
you know the origin of puckered sleeves? It was simply
this: The Countess of Dudley—one of the most beautiful
women in England, by-the-by—was invited to a dinner one
night, and was expecting to shine in a very elegant costume,
which was being made especially for the occasion. When the
countess was about to dress, her maid informed her that the
dressmaker had not yet sent home the costume. The countess
was in despair. What could she do? She wrote a note to the
delinquent, demanding that the dress be sent immediately,
finished or unfinished. It came within an hour—unfinished. The countess felt bound to don it, as several society
papers had already expatiated upon the wonderful design.
The sleeves were only tacked in. The countess was not
daunted. She took a needle and hastily sewed in the sleeves
—so hastily, indeed, that over each shoulder the material
puckered and stood up in alarming folds. She wore the
dress as it was, however. She knew she could wear any-

thing. A week from that time puckered sleeves were all the rage in London.'

"The milliner blushed with shame at this new instance of female weakness. 'Do you know who originated high-heeled boots?' she asked. 'Oh, that woman has a great deal to answer for, I can tell you! It was the Marquise de Pompadour. She was so small, and it was the fashion to be so tall, that she invented high heels, in a fit of desperation. That lady also originated the black patches which were so fashionable in the French court, and which people suppose to-day that the ladies wore in order to heighten the brilliancy of their complexion. They were thus simply in imitation of La Pompadour. She had an aggravating pimple on her cheek, of which she tried hard to get rid. All her efforts were unavailing. She covered the offending growth with black plaster, and set the fashion. Anne of Austria introduced the fashion of short sleeves. She was not a beautiful woman, but her arms were magnificent, and in the same spirit with which Katisha expatiates on the beauty of her left shoulder-blade, Anne of Austria resolved to exhibit her arms. Short sleeves were almost unknown before her time. Marie Antoinette had masses of exquisite hair, and the huge coiffures and outlandish designs which are so much ridiculed to-day were simply the result of that fact. She could do nothing else with her hair, as there was so much of it. But her ladies imitated her, and actually bought false hair in order to reach a proper standard of perfection. Fashions originate in the most ridiculous way. It is absurd to say that one person sets the fashion. She may have a great deal to do with it, but she is not alone in her empire over her sex. The Princess of Wales does a great deal, but she is aided by the Countess of Dudley, Lady Randolph Churchill, and the Marchioness of Kildare. In Paris, it is an acknowledged fact, that at the present day the demi-monde exert considerable influence over the fashion. I could mention at least a dozen instances all illustrative of the fact that fashions are the result of accident and of accident merely—but I won't do it—no, I won't do it,' and the little lady plied her needle in silence."

Of late I have seen a merited rebuke to women for their fashionable follies, in his playful vein, but all the more scathing from its good humor, by Professor David Swing ; and another by a leading lawyer of Boston, who declares that women do not dress so much to please men, but to escape the criticism or excite the envy of each other. I am afraid we must admit that this is nearer the truth than we like to confess. The attacks of men upon the foibles and faults of women are rapidly multiplying, and will do good. What one sex sincerely and seriously disapproves, the other will erelong relinquish. Until recently, women were not in a position of sufficient independence freely to state their opinions concerning the faults of men. Indeed, they are not now, but we rejoice to believe that within fifty years property will be jointly controlled by husband and wife, at which time she will speak her real mind with a clearness never before deemed consistent with the peace of her Home-Jerusalem. Any fashion or frivolity in women which men will not tolerate will rapidly disappear, and *vice versa*. In these days when the drink and tobacco habits are being so steadily frowned upon by women as a class, those who indulge in them can but feel that they stem a tide of public sentiment unknown twenty years since, and by a blessed law of compensation, men are holding up the mirror before women that we may see " oursels as ithers see us." I can but admire and honor every young man who, by fearless but courteously uttered criticism, adds his mite to the chorus that some day " will from mony a folly free us, and foolish notion."

No woman can really win in the world's thickening battle who is not, first of all, obedient to the decalogue of natural law, " written in our members." There is no mistaking its utterances as they sound from the ever-radiant Sinai of physiology and hygiene.

Reverently let me try to write them down, having, alas, learned most of them from old Father Penalty, the severest of all pedagogues.

1. Let the dress be such as will impose no ligature upon any part of the body, nor in anywise restrict the freedom, naturalness, and perfect equilibrium of all its members. Let it be equally distributed over the entire figure, without excrescences or furbelows, and carefully adapted to the season.

2. Let the functions of digestion be normally preserved by the use of the simplest foods, into which enter the elements of nutrition suited to the season, and by a careful, physiological study of the conditions of their healthful maintenance.

3. Let the only drink be water, hot or cold, and milk. Never drink at meals, and never drink ice-water at all.

4. Let the sponge-bath be a daily means of grace.

5. Let God's pure, fresh air have full access to your room, especially at night.

6. Let exercise in the open air be **your daily habit, and** cultivate athletic sports.

7. Let brain-work be dispensed with after tea, and insist on eight hours sleep in twenty-four.

8. Remember the Sabbath day to keep it holy. In the six days thou shalt labor, but in them do all thy work. If the Sabbath is necessarily a day of brain-work—as to public speakers, Christian workers, etc.—take one day in seven for rest or recreation, as the surest means to a useful life and hale old age.

9. Give your soul up to faith. Believe in God, in immortality, in human brotherhood, in the sure triumph of everything pure and good.

10. Habituate yourself to prayer. Let it be the pulse of your whole life; so natural to you that your spirit turns to the Star of Bethlehem as steadily as turns the needle to the polar star.

I am not gifted in divination and will not attempt to cast your horoscope, brave girls of the new America, evermore marching forward to storm the Castle Ignorance, as well as Castle Indolence, but I do not fear to predict an absolutely happy, a most winning, and a thoroughly successful life to whomsoever will obey these ten commandments. To write of them severally is not my purpose. But to lay down some simple rules relative to the daily conduct of life, is a part of my scheme in talking to you of "How to Win." For we must build our strong foundations on the solid bed rock of natural law. Though our foreheads are lifted toward the sky, our feet are firmly planted on the earth. This body is, in a sense, the universe to us. We get no light save that which comes through this strange skylight of the brain. The "man wonderful" lives in a "house beautiful," and it is all in all to him. It was meant to be his perfect instrument and not his prison. Perfect obedience to its laws would make him the true microcosm—the mirror of the universe—nay, of its Creator. The blessed word "health" once literally meant "holiness," and that means simply "wholeness." This body of ours was meant to be the temple of the Holy Spirit, but enemies have taken possession of it and dimmed or wellnigh extinguished the shekinah. A sound mind cannot exist except in a sound body. The Saxons had a saying that "every man has lain on his own trencher," and it is not only true that "the man who drinks beer thinks beer," but "he who eats swine thinks swine," bristles and all. Good old Dr. Peter Akers—of the Peter Cartwright school of preachers, a saint still lingering with us, I believe—says he would like to offer as a fitting oblation to the devil, " a hog stuffed with tobacco in an alcohol gravy." For my own part I have formed a settled conviction that the world is fed too much. Pastries, cakes, hot bread, rich gravies, pickles, pepper-sauces, salads, tea and coffee are discarded from my bill of fare, and I firmly believe they will be from the recipes of the twentieth century. Entire wheat flour bread, vegetables, fruit, fowl, fish, with a little beef and mutton, and water as the chief drink, will distill, in the alembic of the digestive organs, into pure, rich, feverless blood, electric but steady nerves, and brains whose chief delight will be to think God's thoughts after Him.

May the high thinking that consorts best with plain living be a well-known "way to win" among the maidens of America, is my New Year benediction on them all.

CHAPTER VIII.

THE LAW OF HABIT.

That which has been done once is easier done the second time. Repetition is the only basis of perfection. Patient continuance in well-doing conducts by a straight path to glory, honor, and immortality.

From the raw material of truth set forth in those three sentences, destiny is manufactured, and if I were rich enough, I would emblazon them on the mirror of every girl in Christendom.

Since 1874 I have been a steady student of the law of habit—I had well-nigh said the law of fate. I have seen it slowly, gently, imperceptibly wrap men round and round in its close winding-sheet, as if they were Egyptian mummies. So quietly was all this done that they never knew their bondage until the first faint movement toward a better life, when, behold, their helplessness recalled the Indian-tortured hunter perpendicularly planted in the ground with earth packed around him even to the lips. A miracle of faith has rescued some of these ; but a study of years compels the admission that not more than five in one hundred inebriates, gamblers, or libertines are ever permanently reformed. The thoughtless boy, cigar in mouth, playing cards "just for fun," and a little later with a glass of beer as the stake, hiding all these things from his mother, saying to himself, "I'll quit this after a while, but I want to sow my wild oats;" the idle, spendthrift youth with fondness only for the vile company where his worst passions can be gratified; the besotted man, sold under sin, accursed of God and his own conscience and his fellow-men—these are the piteous object lessons that have taught me the supreme power of habit over human destiny. But I saw that the tendency to repeat the same act and the greater ease with which this is done the second time than the first, and the third time than the second, is the key to paradise as well as pandemonium. I saw the slow, unerring, unfailing plan of God, by which our habits may become our step-ladder to saintship. And I said to my own heart in the presence of many a bloated inebriate what now I whisper, dear girls, to you: *No evil habit, however small, shall have dominion over me.* For I am free to say I have set out for saintship and nothing less, though only God knows so well as I how long the road and how far off the goal. Go to now, and let us have a sacred emulation in this slow, steady climb after good habits. I take it for granted that the law of repetition has confirmed you immovably already in the habit of chaste and reverent language, so that you would involuntarily stop your ears in presence of vulgar or blasphemous words. One's language is so thoroughly a part of one's own inmost self that in my hearing a young man whom I had befriended and who meant me no disrespect, once crimsoned every sentence with an oath, and when repeatedly called to account he kept repeating, "I beg your pardon, I had no idea of swearing—it says itself." By the same law, I know of men as well as women who would as soon try to grasp an object by turning their fingers backward instead of forward, as they would use vile language or profane the name of God. They don't know how it is done. But there are doubtful pleasantries and witty irreverencies "into the habit" of which many good people have fallen. Whose vocabulary would bear the electric light of publicity from one year's end to another? But a Christian ought to stand this test. Let us raise a standard right here. Get out your memorandum-book and pledge yourself hereby "with God's help":

1. *Resolved, That I will utter no word and convey no thought unworthy of a Christian disciple.*

Remember that this means to put away all "evil speaking." Ah, that is hewing to the line. So let it be, no matter where the chips fly. "In her tongue is the law of kindness." If we have not formed this habit we are still word-scavengers, not ready for the society of the true household of faith, not trained in its etiquette nor cultured so as to feel at home within its blessed family circle. I do not mean that this gentleness of speech excludes analysis of character and commentary upon word and deed. Then would society become a Chinese picture without perspective and without atmosphere, our perceptions of moral distinctions would be dulled, and the faculty of criticism dwarfed. We may pass upon the acts of others as right or wrong, we may even pronounce upon their personal tendencies as good or bad, but we must, in every debatable case, give to their *motive* the benefit of a doubt. So high an authority in criticism as the sculptor-poet, William Story, once set out to prove that Judas Iscariot may have been determined to force from Christ the use of His miraculous powers by placing Him in a position where death was the only alternative, that thus the Jews might throw off the Roman yoke and the Messiah reign as was His right! You have all heard the story of a charitably-minded old lady of whom a gainsaying youth declared that he'd wager that she would defend his Satanic majesty in case his character were attacked in her hearing, and drew from the kind old saint the declaration that "if Christians would only imitate the perseverance of the devil this world would soon be saved." She must have been related to the one whose sons were sent to State prison, and whose friends declared that "Aunt Heavenly Mind would find some good even in that." Sure enough, when told of the sentence, she mildly said, "Well, it'll be a dretful comfort to know where them boys be of a night." We may laugh at all this, but who doubts the superior "live-with-able-ness" of such characters as compared with the curled-lipped fault-finders for whom nothing on earth is good enough except their own delectable selves. We are to "do unto others as we would they should do unto us." This is the basis of all good habits pertaining to society. Now, you and I do not expect or desire that our character and deeds shall pass without commentary. That would be to covet living burial. Very well, since we are imperfect, no true commentary upon us can be made without involving criticism which, however just, it might pain us to hear. Do we then wish to gag the human race that it shall not speak out its mind concerning us? What standards would it have upon that plan? What chance to develop keen discrimination and hold up illustrations now for imitation, and now for warning? It seems to me we need more criticism instead of less. But it should be candid, courteous, kindly, and from high motives. Coleridge gave us the divine canon of criticism when he said we were to *look* for the *beauties* in a picture or a character. Instead of that how often have we heard a long discussion of some famous, and on the whole, benignant character, with not one appreciative word from first to last, and in neighborhood gossip it is the same. Let us, then, listen to ourselves carefully, and see if we have been so churlish or one-sided as to speak only of faults in our analysis, be it only of a child, a servant, or a dog. We cannot afford to form the habit of detraction, and go about one-eyed, forever seeing half. The *nil admirari* school of talkers, writers, and livers would soon transform this very tolerable world into a veritable slough of despond if they had it all to themselves. There is a crude, youthful period when this *rôle* is thought to indicate wisdom, but as life mellows us we ought to form a habit of humility which would lead us to esteem others better than ourselves.

Every considerate word we utter concerning those about us; every time we give them the benefit of a doubt in our judgment of their motive; every time we take occasion to couple with our demurrer from their position some saving clause of appreciation, we are habituating ourselves to that charity which "suffereth long and is kind;" that heavenly love which alone can make us meet for heavenly company.

"Time doth the impression deeper make
As streams their channels deeper wear."

Just as you now play without the music and do not think what notes you strike, though once you picked them out by slow and patient toil, so if you begin of set purpose, you will learn the law of kindness in utterance so perfectly, that it will be second nature to you, and make more music in your life than all the songs the sweetest voice has ever sung.

There is another resolution I would earnestly enforce on your attention. It was freshly brought to mine at a church union meeting of ladies in " my ain familiar town" during the week of prayer. Four churches were represented, and eleven ladies either spoke or prayed, of whom seven were Methodists. As I conducted the meeting I can speak freely of but six among those Methodist ladies, and I will say that the six Doctors of Divinity by whose presence our regular church prayer-meeting is enriched and blest could not have spoken better. The manner of these ladies was thoroughly gentle and womanly, but as completely self-possessed as it would have been in their own parlors. The thoughts they presented were among the loftiest, tenderest, and most strengthening that I have ever heard ; while the language was chaste, idiomatic, and pictorial. Why were they thus " at home" in the Lord's house ? Because they were made to feel at home in girlhood ; their pleasant voices had always been welcome in the circle of prayer ; they had been coveted witnesses for Christ since the day they joined the church. The other ladies who sat by in silence were just as good women and potentially just as gifted, but they lacked the sense of liberty and the sanctuary education. By the law of contrast, their silence reminded me of the reply made by a gallant British officer to the question, " How is it that you can ride up to the cannon's mouth and never flinch ?" He answered, " *Sir, it is the courage of having done the thing.*"

Here comes in that **changeless** law of habit, blest or

blighting, according to our personal relation with it. Upon it let us base our *Resolution 2. I will religiously cultivate the power to speak and pray in the meetings of my church, God being my helper.*

Happily now, the churches nearly all see their duty to the silent two thirds so long uncomplainingly suppressed. Perhaps the law of self-preservation has also somewhat to do with this growing liberality of sentiment. I was very much amused by the remark of a young man at our church prayer-meeting a few evenings ago. When all were, by request, giving their special reasons for gratitude, he said, "Well, I thank God that I did not come on the scene of action until the days when women spoke in meeting." Now it is your good fortune, young Americans, to live, move, and have your being at a time when the world is full of just such brotherly souls as this University student in Evanston. The old difficulties about interpreting St. Paul have vanished. I once heard a pastor say at the South, "I reckon I put my own narrow notions into the Bible and then proceeded to think they were inspired." In that pithy sentence is comprised, to my mind, every word of exegesis that has proclaimed the subjection of those who were last at Christ's cross, first at His sepulchre, and first to proclaim His resurrection. "The letter killeth; the spirit giveth life." To be sure, Paul says in so many words, "It is not permitted unto them to speak." But all the same Miriam led the song of triumph; Deborah was raised up of God to be not only a judge but a prophetess; Huldah was a prophetess in Jerusalem, instructing Josiah the king; Anna when she entered the house of God, "gave thanks unto the Lord and spake of Him to all them that looked for redemption in Jerusalem"—thus not only exhorting but publicly praying in presence of the whole congregation and in the very temple of God ; and Priscilla " expounded the way of God more perfectly" to the eloquent preacher Apollos. Besides all this, St. Paul himself, in that same portentous Epistle of Corinthians, explicitly prescribes the conditions under which woman shall both pray and prophesy, and yet he says, " It is not permitted unto them to speak," and " It is a shame for women to speak in the church," and " I suffer not a woman to teach." In view of the plain facts and undoubted precedents of the Bible for woman's doing all these things, enforced by the august authority of Christ, who uttered no word against the sacred ministries of woman, what are we to conclude ? It seems to me, and I know this but echoes the opinion of some of our best and wisest pastors, that Paul, who was " all things to all men that by all means he might save the most," deemed it expedient for the infant Church, among the many pitfalls in its way, to *con*form while it endeavored to *re*form ; and that those fateful words " It is not permitted " and the rest are simple statements of fact as to the customs of that day. He could not have meant that God's law did not permit, for no such utterance can be found between the two lids of the Bible, and the examples given are all the other way.

"Every woman that prayeth or prophesieth with her head uncovered dishonoreth her head, for that is even all one as if she were shaven. Judge in yourselves : is it comely that a woman pray unto God uncovered ?"

But in ten thousand school-rooms and homes Christian women daily pray to God with " heads uncovered," and not even the most literal theologian considers that they have "dishonored their heads" (whatever that may be). But if they really have not dishonored them, then the whole system of literalism falls. If it be not a sin when we fail to wash each other's feet at the sacrament, although Christ said explicitly, "Ye ought to wash one another's feet, for I have given you an example that you should do as I have done to you," then we have the highest sanction for exalting the spirit of the New Testament and ceasing to insist so much upon its letter.

CHAPTER IX.

HOW DO YOU TREAT YOUR LAUNDRESS?

"Permit my congratulations upon the choice selection you have made," sneered Adonis, as his critical glance fell upon the title of this chapter. I could not be offended; the subject has few fascinations I admit, and yet I choose to offer it for your consideration. The thistle is a common sort of plant, but as well worth studying, perhaps, as pinks or violets. Besides, we have a surfeit nowadays of choice alliterative themes. Indeed, the more I think about it the more I am disposed to plume myself upon my subject—to which let me now address myself.

Nocturne and I were walking down the street, talking with animation about two beautiful engravings of the famous statues, "Night and Morning," which had that day been given her. Somehow everything chimed with my mood, which was a very pleasant one. The day was splendid; the air was inspiration, and in the exultant spirit which these influences gave, I dared to think of the serene, triumphant face of "Morning" as but faintly shadowing forth the companionships of that wonderful life which hastens to be mine. Far up in the fathomless blue that marvellous face seemed outlined, the faintness of the limning only adding to the intenseness of my gaze. Just then a heavy step fell on the gravelled sidewalk; she was crossing the street not a yard ahead of us—my laundress.

When a painful contrast smites us we are apt to think.

There was no mistaking the identity of this person who had so ruthlessly put a radiant reverie to flight; no mistaking the heavy mouth, retreating forehead, and upturned nose; the faded shawl and worn-out hood; the rounded shoulders and clumsy step. No, the badges were upon her, branded into the face by life-long consciousness of inferiority; by a thousand stifled ambitions and thwarted purposes; certified by the mode of that life and its result.

Nocturne turned in at her own gate and ran lightly up the steps to her own door. I paused a moment, pleasing myself by contemplation of the grace which every attitude and movement of my charming friend revealed—from the sprightly nod which she bestowed upon me as we parted, to the last, tripping step which carried her beyond my sight.

How great a gulf is fixed between those two, I thought, as I walked on. Life has no mystery darker than this. What would Eve say, I wonder, to these her daughters? and for which would her motherly heart conceive the tenderest love? Doubtless, with that wonderful instinct of motherhood, she would love her best whom Fortune had most disregarded.

Nocturne and Bridget may fairly serve as types of their respective classes. What good gifts he dispenses to the first! The commonplace necessities of every day come not to her as such, but wear some amiable disguise. And this disguise is so complete that hunger—if I may utter a word so harsh in ears polite—is made the cause of an enjoyment which, although we are not wont to say so, is keen and by no means unrefined; while to thirst, its unromantic congener, the unhygienic world owes its relish for the fragrant Mocha and the famous cups "which cheer but not inebriate."

The elegant appointments of a table where damask conceals mahogany, and where china, silver, and cut-glass support viands culled from every zone, and prepared with a skill which an extensive literature of cook-books and centuries of practice contribute to perfect, cannot very vividly remind one of the physical demand which sends the beggar from door to door, or the cabin where poverty dispenses, at the hands of the hard-working mother, a boiled potato seasoned with salt to each of the clamorous "childer." And the merry jest or spirited rejoinder, the tinkle of spoons and of laughter, which form the accompaniments to breakfast, dinner, and tea in the houses of ease and elegance, are very remotely allied to those sounds which betoken the rapid imbibition of fluids and the energetic mastication of solids at the tables of the poor. In like manner the selection of styles and grouping of colors in dress, considered so essential by those composing what we call the "better classes," is so far removed from the careful contrivances of poverty that we can hardly think the underlying need the same.

Bridget, after great deliberation and frequent consultation with sympathizing friends, concludes that she must have a woollen shawl in order that she may not catch her death's cold when she goes to "mass." So, taking her wallet with its hoarded treasure of ten dollars, she wends her way to town. She enters one store after another in pursuit of the desired pattern and price—both being extremely difficult to find. She is flippantly accosted by lily-handed, high-collared clerks; is spitefully entreated by the same young gentlemen when she meekly suggests, "Av ye plaze, couldn't ye let this go a dollar chaper to the likes o' me?" is swept aside with an imperious gesture while a more attractive customer is served; is jostled on the sidewalk, elbowed off the crossing, angrily reprimanded the third time that she counts her money before paying for her purchase when it is finally made, and returns to her cheerless home with an assured conviction that this world isn't a very pleasant place, and her shawl not such a wonderful prize after all, though praised be St. Patrick that she got it at all.

Doesn't your heart ache for her, just a little, under your broadcloth and velvet? Well, if it doesn't, it ought to ache, that's all.

Nocturne sees a pretty fur collar or a handsome cloak at Blank's, and reflecting that her last winter's sack is getting out of style, tells papa—very prettily, of course—that she will be obliged to him for a treasury note of rather high denomination, and upon papa's placing it in her hand with his usual generous air, *she* wends *her* way to town. Of course she goes to Blank's—that is the best establishment. Her well-known face secures for her immediate attention. She is a very desirable customer, and has already patronized the firm liberally; but a face and manner like hers would insure every civility, even were she unheralded by an enviable reputation. So the delicate-handed gentlemen vie with each other to pay her honors; the proprietor himself comes forward and amid most assiduous attentions the purchase is made, the elegant little portemonnaie is opened, the bill is paid, the order, "Please send to my street and number," is interrupted by the obsequious acquiescence of the clerks, and Nocturne is bowed out of the store with the profoundest deference. Nocturne and Bridget must both provide for winter, the demand is identical; the mode of meeting that demand, how different!

And yet, when all is said, these are but minor matters. I think more sadly of my laundress for other griefs than these.

A favorite servant once said to me as she wiped the perspiration from her face after a hard day's work, "I wonder if you ever think what a poor life it is for us who must be always managing to get a bit to eat and something to wear? We must be always working for the body and doing nothing for the soul, and yet after a while the body'll go away from us, but the soul, you know, never goes away."

I cannot forget the words, and memory still brings back with sad distinctness the plaintive tones in which poor, patient Margaret said, "The soul, you know, will never go away." Pitiful as it is to be hungry and cold; painfully industrious as a woman must be to ward off cold and hunger by the labors of the laundry, there is something still more pitiful in the life-long hunger of unfed capacities, and the stupor of faculties unused.

A deformed body is a sad sight, I know; but who shall paint the frightful portrait of a deformed soul? We think but little of it in this world, where things visible so much engross us, but it is none the less true that the screen of a material form delivers us from the hideous spectacle which many an undisguised soul would present.

Weakened by disease; distorted by the life-long grasp of ignorance, scarred in its futile strife with fate; stung by a world's implied contempt—what conception is so terrible as this of a thwarted will, a barren intellect, an outraged sensibility?

For that weary, uncouth woman who broke the spell of my reflections, the torch of history is still unlighted; for her, science reveals no secret; artists evoke from canvas the visions which haunt their dreams, sculptors carve their thoughts in marble, and singers wake from lyre and organ mystic voices to mingle with their own; but these radiant revelations of the beautiful are lavished on more favored lives than hers. I know this is a land of plenty; I know the rich are often generous, and our thoughts are turned toward the poor in every prayer we hear and often in our sermons and our songs. But do we think enough of their great loss in losing throughout all their years the choicest treasures that enrich our own? With what zest do we gather truth after truth into our memories! How keen is our relish for "the quaint and curious volume of forgotten lore;" for the calm and kindly teaching of the wise and good who flourished in past ages! How we please ourselves with song and story; with following the explorer into strange and distant regions, or visiting with the tourist the shrines of learning and of beauty in all lands and centuries, so that we count our books a solace in all trouble and loneliness, and turn to them for comfort when all other sources fail!

But contemplate a life that has no past; that wins from the wisdom of sages, the eloquence of orators, and the inspiration of poets, no comforting suggestion; a life undignified by research—unbeautified by accomplishment! We do well to think with tenderest regret of these for whom no Shakespeare "holds the mirror up to nature's face," no

Wordsworth muses, no Milton sings! But we do better if we work and pray to bring again that golden age of which traditions tell us, when all men's weal shall be each man's care; when the only aristocracy known upon the earth shall be the aristocracy of wisdom; to whose loftiest seat the patient steps of the poorest may certainly attain.

CHAPTER X.

NOVEL-READING

Much as I disliked the restriction then, I am now sincerely thankful that my Puritan father not only commanded me not to read novels, but successfully prohibited the temptation from coming in his children's way. Until I was fifteen years old I never saw a volume of the kind.

"Pilgrim's Progress" was the nearest approach we made, but it seems profanation to refer to that choice English classic in this degenerate connection. (I should add that Rev. Dr. Tefft's "Shoulder Knot" was also early read at our house, in the *Ladies' Repository;* but then that delightful work was an *historical* story, and even my father praised it.)

A kind and garrulous seamstress, who declared that this law of our household was "a shame," told us what she could remember of "The Children of the Abbey," and finally brought in, surreptitiously, "Jane Eyre" and "Thaddeus of Warsaw." But the glamor of those highly seasoned pages was unhealthful, and made "human nature's daily food," the common pastoral life we led, and nature's soothing beauty seem so tame and tasteless that the revulsion was my life's first sorrow. How evanescent and unreal was the pleasure of such reading; a sort of spiritual hasheesh-eating with hard and painful waking; a benumbing of the healthful, every-day activities ; a losing of so much that was simple and sweet, to gain so little that was, at best, a fevered and fantastic vision of utter unreality. In all the years since then I have believed that novel-writing, save for some high, heroic, moral aim, while the most diversified, is the most unproductive of all industries. The young people who read the greatest quantity of novels know the least, are the dullest in aspect, and the most vapid in conversation. The flavor of individuality has been burned out of them. Always imagining themselves in an artificial relation to life, always content to look through their author's glasses, they become as commonplace as pawns upon a chess-board. "Sir, we had good talk!" was Sam Johnson's highest praise of those he met. But any talk save the dreariest commonplace and most tiresome reiteration is impossible with the regulation reader of novels or player of games. And this is, in my judgment, because God, by the very laws of mind, must punish those who *kill* time instead of *cultivating* it. For time is the stuff that life is made of ; the crucible of character, the arena of achievement, and woe **to** those who fritter it away. They cannot help paying great nature's penalty, and "mediocre," "failure," or "imbecile" will surely be stamped upon their foreheads. Therefore I would have each generous youth and maiden say to every story-spinner, except the few great names that can be counted on the fingers of one hand : I really cannot patronize your wares, and will not furnish you my head for a football, or my fancy for a sieve. By writing these books you get money, and a fleeting, unsubstantial fame, but by reading them I should turn my possibility of success in life to the certainty of failure. *Myself plus time* is the capital stock with which the good heavenly Father has pitted me against the world to see if I can gain some foothold. I cannot afford to be a mere spectator. I am a wrestler for the laurel in life's Olympian games. I can make history, why should I maunder in a hammock and read the endless repetitions of romance ? No, find yourself a cheaper patron, for I count myself too valuable for the sponge-like use that you would put me to.

Nay, I would have our young people reach a higher key than this. Because of life's real story with its mystery and pathos; because of the romance that crowds into every year; the plot that thickens daily, and the tragedy that lies a little way beyond; because of Christ and His kingdom—the mightiest drama of the ages, let us be up and doing with a heart for any fate. Humanity is worth our while, to love, to bless, to die for if need be.

> "The cause that lacks assistance,
> The wrong that needs resistance,
> The future in the distance
> And the good that we can do,"

make up the truest epic and train the noblest heroes. Achievement, which is growth's condition, ought to be the bread of life to us, the tireless inspiration of each full day of honest toil. God meant this to be so, for only thus do we cease chasing about for happiness, and find blessedness instead.

CHAPTER XI.

WOMAN'S OPPORTUNITY IN JOURNALISM.

IN the steady advance of journalism woman has borne no inconspicuous part.

Since Lydia Maria Child founded her magazine for children, Lydia H. Sigourney wrote verses for the *Hartford Press*, Margaret Fuller furnished book notices for Horace Greeley's New York *Tribune*, or Harriet Beecher Stowe sent to the *National Era* the most celebrated serial of the century, "Uncle Tom's Cabin," woman has been an important fact in the profession.

Her opportunity in journalism as everywhere else comes not by revolution but by evolution. When journalism was on a purely material plane she could have but little place within its borders, but the spiritualizing process which it has undergone has opened its doors to her, and she has demonstrated her ability to meet most of its various demands.

When I think of Madame Ida Pfeiffer, Lady Duff Gordon, the wife of Sir Samuel Baker, and others like them; when I notice whole libraries of foreign travel from the pens of women, and their growing opportunity for out-door life, athletic sports, and rational modes of dress; I have great hopes of their capacity to meet every requirement of the most varied and adventurous journalistic career. If a woman like Miss Minnie Morgan, of New York, can be a first-class live-stock reporter, with all the hardships and discomforts of such an occupation, we may fairly predict that the Mollie Pitchers, the Di Vernons, and the Rosa Bonheurs of journalism, will yet appear, although woman's grandest journalistic opportunity is to be sought in higher, if not wider, fields. For here, as everywhere, she seems destined to soften asperities, to sublimate coarseness, to eliminate the last reminder of barbarity. She will thus supply the precise elements the lack of which we now lament. Being refined, she will add fineness; being compassionate, she will add compassion; being conscientious, she will add conscience in a larger measure to the "writing up" of the world's great diurnal history. Less space will be given to the prize-fight and more to the prize poem; the murder trial will be condensed that the philanthropic convention may gain a wider hearing; the wholesale verdict against political opponents merely because they are such will be modified by an attempt to show some faint approach to justice, even toward partisan enemies; of personalities there will be more rather than less, but the delineation of helpful lives and how they came to be so will largely replace the biographies of successful gamblers, whether in Wall Street stocks or Western faro-banks; and I seriously doubt if any woman journalist will ever stoop to say to another, even behind the mask of the editorial "we," that she "tells absolute lies." It is time that a standard were lifted in unfaltering hands against this growing evil of wholesale verbal venom, for if it be true that "as a man readeth in his newspaper so is he," it is equally true that so speaketh he. The incessant criticisms and harsh judgments of the press are doing more than any other one cause, except original sin, to lower the tone of common conversation in respect to that loftiest but, alas, most evanescent grace—sweet charity.

The work of women will receive such recognition as is not now to be expected, for the pride of sex, which makes whatever men do of especial interest to men, will magnify in the view of the lady reporter the importance of helping on all the enterprises in which women are engaged.

In brief, woman has now the opportunity to do for journalism what she long ago accomplished for literature—to drive out the Fieldings and the Smolletts from its temple; to replace sentimentality by sentiment; to frown upon coarse jests, debasing innuendoes, and irreverent witticisms; to come into its realm as

> "A creature not too bright or good
> For human nature's daily food,
> And yet, a spirit, fair and bright,
> With something of an angel's light."

The difference between the smoking and drawing-room cars on a railway train illustrates that between average journalism as it is and as it will be when men and women sit at their desks in the same editorial and reportorial sanctums. One is full of fumes, the other of perfumes; one is a small section of chaos, the other of creation; and all because one is denaturalizing, the other natural. The "Club" will cut a smaller and the "Household" a larger figure in the journalism of the future; indeed the difference between bachelor's hall and home is, in reality, the one we are now trying to analyze. No truth, theological, political, or economic, can be seen in its entirety until the stereoscopic view from the two angles of vision, the masculine and feminine, give it precision and bring it out into bold relief.

Read Kate Upson Clark's "Helping Hand" department as it appears week by week in the Philadelphia *Press*, and see how much may be done to uplift working-women and to make them feel that in the great daily paper they have an intelligent and trusty friend. Read the "Woman's Kingdom," first edited by Elizabeth Boynton Harbert, in the Chicago *Inter-Ocean*, and see what has been done by that high-class daily to broaden the outlook of the home people and to incite young women to wide and noble aims. Read the *Times-Democrat* and the *Picayune*, of New Orleans, both owned and one conducted by women, and recognize in them the chief evangels to our sisters of the South. Clearly enough, woman's opportunity in journalism is just what it is in the great world. She has a *rôle* peculiar to herself. The niche she is to fill would remain empty but for her arrival. If the best journalist be likened unto Apollo, "the lord of the unerring bow," then she is his sister Diana, standing by his side, and if the worst be likened to the "Beast," then together they are "Beauty and the Beast." Rather let us call them Ganymede and Hebe, cup-bearers of news-nectar to the gods of counting-room and parlor. They will look best side by side. He has special advantages, amply offset by gifts of hers impossible for him to gain. She would hardly jump from the deck of the ship that rescued the steamer Oregon's passengers recently and swim to the news tug with the account of that great casualty, as did an enterprising reporter for the New York press. But peace hath her victories no less than war, and calm no less than storm. To sketch a scene in the Senate chamber so that its vividness shall reproduce both individuality and environment before our eyes, commend me to Mary Clemmer; and to reproduce the fine sympathy of a conference of charities, or a temperance convention, so that it shall kindle that of the reader, give me Mary Bannister Willard or Mary Allen West. In all first-class descriptive writing by women journalists there is a pictorial quality by which their work can usually be recognized, and a photographic clearness in their personal portraitures.

The daily press, which has become already the people's university, is to be largely the pulpit and the forum of the future. Here woman has a place to stand, a pulpit ready from which no ecclesiastic edict can exclude her, and from which she can comfort humanity's heart, "as one whom his mother comforteth;" and in this forum can her weapons of argument be sharpened for the time when "Portia" shall become a flesh and blood creation in halls of justice.

Journalism is the paradise of the philanthropist. From the platform he reaches hundreds, but through the press hundreds of thousands. It is estimated that about twenty-five years are requisite for an idea to "get around" and find its equilibrium in average brains; but the daily newspaper can, if it will, reduce this period to ten years. The propaganda, by this process, goes not at stage-coach but at lightning speed. To fuse public sentiment into **sympathy and weld it into organization, we must have the** glowing forge of daily journalism.

The larger the audience, the **more immediate and the**

more homogeneous is the impression made. But the press has the largest and most frequent audience in Christendom. Mindful of this, the Woman's Christian Temperance Union has for one of its chief plans to appoint a "press superintendent" in every town, who shall keep the local editor informed of temperance arguments and progress. Our national superintendent, Mrs. Esther T. Housh, of Brattleboro, Vt., the gifted editor of the *Woman's Magazine*, sends out bulletins by tens of thousands to State presidents of the Woman's Christian Temperance Union, and they, in turn, to their lists of local reporters; while for the large cities, "patent side" papers, etc., Miss Julia Ames, of Chicago, condenses the temperance news once a week, besides sending, on special occasions, an Associated Press telegram. Here is one of the newest and amplest fields in the whole range of newspaper apprenticeship.

As in the world at large, so in the world of journalism, woman's favorite specialty will always be some phase of religious, educational, reformatory, or philanthropic work, or some topic relating to the home. Nearly all the papers treating of humanitarian enterprises are already either conducted, or largely influenced, by women journalists, and, as every reader knows, women do some of the best work on the religious press. Scan the pages of the *Independent*, the *Christian Union*, the *Witness*, the *Sunday-school Times*, and the numerous church papers for women's names "revered, beloved" at the firesides of the nation, while educational journals have, like the many-sided *Chautauquan*, shown them a brother's hospitality. The missionary papers conducted by women are an epoch in literature ; and the temperance papers of which they control the finance as well as the editing, are becoming a mighty power for good. To conduct a paper successfully requires business talent of the highest order, and nowhere have women proved their gifts more conspicuously than in this field. They have saved the day for many a languishing enterprise, and in missionary circles have repeatedly paid expenses and had a handsome margin left for the cause. As a white-ribbon woman I am proud to say for the *Union Signal* (whose honored founder is Mrs. Matilda B. Carse, of Chicago) that our lively sixteen-page weekly not only pays its way but has recently paid a dividend of four per cent to the large constituency of temperance women who constitute its stockholders.

The best proof of woman's opportunity in journalism is the women themselves and the work they have wrought. Among the most valued perquisites of my ten years' peregrinations as a temperance organizer, I count the personal acquaintance, and in many instances the friendship, of a majority of these gifted bread-winners. If called upon to name the chief half dozen among them, I should say Grace Greenwood, Gail Hamilton, Mary Mapes Dodge, Mary L. Booth, Jennie June, and Lucy Stone. Each has an assured place in the annals of our time, and while brilliantly successful in some form of journalism, almost all are equally well known in other fields—especially the field of authorship. The phenomenal success of Miss Gilder, editor of the *Critic*, entitles her to the same rank, were her work not so recent as to be still unrecognized by the public at large. The most distinguished journalists we have lost are Mary Clemmer, Jane Gray Swisshelm, and Sarah Josepha Hale.

Kate Sanborn would rank high if she would but join the ranks instead of writing books, and Laura C. Holloway had hardly a peer while connected with the Brooklyn press. Sarah K. Bolton for point and compactness of style is *sui generis*, and our journalistic ranks cannot afford to lose any of these, even to gain the helpful books they are now writing.

Mrs. Frank Leslie, of New York, is holding with firm hand the great enterprises founded by her husband; Mrs. Nicholson, of the New Orleans *Picayune*, has already been referred to; Mrs. Myra Bradwell, of Chicago, has made the *Legal News* a high authority as well as a complete financial success; Margaret Buchanan Sullivan has hardly a superior among men or women as a "general utility" writer for the daily press, and would have the same reputation among readers that she has among journalists were not her work largely impersonal; and to this list might be added a score of names, full of interest to all women alike, by reason of their character and work. Mary Lowe Dickinson and Susan Hale of *Lend a Hand*, the new magazine of philanthropy founded in Boston by Edward Everett Hale; Ella Farnum Pratt, who may be said to have created that charming magazine for children, *Wide Awake;* Lucia Gilbert Runkle, the sparkling occasional correspondent of the New York *Tribune;* Marion McBride, of the Cleveland press; Alice Stone Blackwell, now on the editorial staff of the *Woman's Journal;* Fanny Casseday Duncan, the "wise woman" of the Louisville *Courier-Journal;* Mrs. Florence Adkinson and May Wright Sewell, of Indianapolis, that city of bright women, all merit "special mention."

We are all proud to regard Mrs. Mary A. Livermore, Elizabeth Stuart Phelps, Susan Coolidge, and Kate Field as in some sense journalists, though their greater achievements in other lines have caused them to be classified elsewhere; and the same might be said of Julia Ward Howe, Louise Chandler Moulton, and the lamented "H. H."

Nor do we forget that Susan B. Anthony and Elizabeth Cady Stanton have been editors—and no brighter ones are on the list. It is recorded to the everlasting credit of the former that after she was forty years old she subjected herself to the calamitous experiences of lyceum lecturing that she might earn ten thousand dollars not legally owed by her but which she regarded as a newspaper debt of honor, and paid to the last farthing. With these two pioneers of "women's rights" I must mention their latest allies, Mrs. Duniway, editor of the *New Northwest* in Oregon, and Mrs. Clara Colby, of the *Woman's Tribune*, Nebraska.

As a Western woman I can but feel especial pride in the remarkable success of a young lady, born and reared in a country village of my own State, who has already become the literary editor of one of the oldest daily papers in Boston, and who is undoubtedly the most popular special correspondent who dates her letters from the Hub; I mean Miss Lilian Whiting, of the Boston *Traveller*, daughter of Senator L. D. Whiting, of Tiskilwa, Ill. After a brief apprenticeship in St. Louis, Miss Whiting went to Boston four years ago, without influence, *prestige*, or friends. She asked the *Traveller* people to let her make them a report of some meeting that was to occur, and they wisely consented. She did her work well. It was quite out of the regulation reporter's style, being not only concise and accurate, but vividly reproducing the scene and the actors therein. She worked on patiently, step by step, until now her position is assured.

As I have sat beside this noble gifted girl in her elegant rooms at the Hotel Vendôme; taken account of her entrance into the most exclusive circles, literary and artistic, of Boston and New York; read her letters full of point and piquancy; and asked myself the secret of her success, the answer has been one that young women may wisely ponder: "She has not only ability, but what is just as vital, she has availability; she has not only a clear head, but a warm heart; she has not only rare talent, but unequalled courage, consummate perseverance, and relentless industry."

The chief reasons why journalism will always be, next to philanthropy, the most natural and satisfactory vocation of the intellectual woman seem to me to be these:

1. The "Woman Question" is settled in the "Republic of Letters." Both sexes stand on the same footing, with equal pay and preferment for equal work and success.

2. One is in good company. Journalists as a class are among the brightest, kindest, and most companionable of earth's inhabitants.

3. There is less likelihood of a discontinuance of one's income and a break in one's career on account of marriage, than in most pursuits, for pen and ink plus ideas makes a handy kit of tools, well suited to the surroundings of a home. Even Whitelaw Reid dictates his editorials and corrects the proof by telephone from his elegant up-town mansion; and the progress of invention will constantly improve the adjustments between office and home, so that no

woman who writes with nib inevitable and ink indelible will find her journalistic occupation gone just because there is written in her marriage certificate the climax chapter of her own life's serial story.

4. Journalism is a calling in which specialties abound. The woman's opportunity in journalism is likely to be greatest who most successfully tills some chosen plot of ground in the great field of literature. Let the selection be made with due deliberation, and then steadfastly adhered to. Reputation is capital of the most substantial sort, and along the crowded street of journalism reputation comes to the specialist first and stays there longest. A specialty in these competitive days is the difference between point and no point; between a dead flat and a clean cut perspective; between the monotonous sea and the sunbright sail. Therefore, with all thy gettings, get a specialty.

5. Journalism is a profession of unbounded usefulness and power. Every generous nature desires to make the earning of an honest living but a means to the higher end of adding to the sum total of human goodness and human happiness. There is no foothold which conducts more surely to this result than that of a newspaper woman. But this enchanted realm is without an "open sesame." It has no spell by which to conjure. The conditions are hard-faced as printer's type, and pointed as a stylographic pen. "*Work your passage*" or you cannot win this port. Begin at the foot of the ladder and climb up round by round or you will not reach this height. Learn your alphabet before you tackle polysyllables. The printer's case is a good place to begin. Accuracy, rapidity, skill in detail, are all as vital to the journalist as to the type-setter; William

Lloyd Garrison studied both arts at a time, so did William D. Howells, Robert Burdette, and a host besides who have become famous. To thousands of aspiring young women, bound to be journalists, I would like to say, as I wish some one had said to me in girlhood, learn the printer's trade, and meanwhile try your hand at writing; you will thus hold one bread-winning implement while you reach out for another. Never wait for something to turn up; take hold of the types, they move the world, and turn them right side up; keep on doing this faithfully, and if you have the gift predicted by your preference, you will slowly and steadily, but surely, win a foothold in the splendid realm of journalism.

CHAPTER XII.

AT WHAT AGE SHALL GIRLS MARRY?

WHEN Théophile Gautier announced it as his intention to write a book, entitled "Travels in Spain," his friends expostulated. "But you have never been there," they said. "Assuredly not," replied the man of fancy; "do you suppose I would spoil my ideal by any such stupidity as that?" Not dissimilar is the unprejudiced relation of the present witness to the subject in hand.

"Who shall decide when doctors disagree?" is not an old saw, but a live question, for in anticipation of this chapter, the writer addressed questions to eight of the most distinguished physicians in America, and their replies, as to the age when girls should marry in our temperate zone, range along the chronological gamut all the way from eighteen to twenty-six. But I am glad to add that the balance of their testimony, and their own emphatic commentary on the text afforded by these figures, is, that a girl's life should be safely beyond the rippling shallows of her half-bewildered "teens," before the Rhone and Arve meet. [Please to observe that I prudently refrain from invidious discrimination as to "which is which" in this aqueous simile.] There are, however, other and more decisive estimates than mere numerals can furnish. Indeed, to have a "head for figures" was never my weakness, hence I would determine the proper marriage age with very little reference to any birthday limitation.

Briefly, then, Sophronisca is too immature to think seriously about a life-long comradeship with Sophroniscus, unless she has been sacredly schooled in every law of God written in her members, and counts obedience to these heavenly voices the key that opens almost every door to a true and happy life. She is too young if she has not learned that

> "No lasting link to bind two souls is wrought,
> When passion takes no deeper cast from thought."

She is too young if she thinks his *rôle* in their new drama is to be that of money-maker and hers of money-spender; too young until she has enough of motherhood's ineffable and sacred instinct to repudiate an alliance which unites her to a man of voluntarily deteriorated physique, and which does not bring to her the same total abstinence from alcoholic and nicotine poison which she brings to it and the same purity for purity. Were she the only one to be considered, she might righteously forgive much, because she loves much; but unless pitifully ignorant and unready for the sacrament of marriage, she will not dare invoke the tremulous, immortal lives of the innocent and lovely, upon conditions that involve deterioration and weakness from the first, and at the last may lead to unutterable misery and shame. I would apply another test: Look at the average fashion-plate, Sophronisca; what is its impression? Do its paniers and high heels, low-necks and hour-glass waists, its top-knot bonnets, artificial attitudes, and simpering faces strike you with mental nausea and spiritual scorn? Then, had you passed a score of years, I would make you out the marriage license were men wise enough to let a woman be justice of the peace.

Let us try another test. Stand at your mirror with a photograph of Sophroniscus in your hand. Look at his forehead and your own. Are you already married to the eyebrows? Have you subjects to talk about that are worth while? Is it hard to start new topics, or does the conversation say itself? Do you enjoy the same books, and like to read aloud in one another's hearing? Does he buy the daily paper when you go on an excursion, and then grow silent for a while, or do you invade the solitude of the masculine intellect by quip and commentary that make him wish to share the great world-picture with you, as he would were his college chum beside him? Companionship is the choicest thing on earth, the rarest, the most valued. For it we seek as eagerly, and, alas, often as fruitlessly, as Diogenes sought for an honest man. It is not like the gauzy robe of admiration, nor the royal purple of passion, but no other fabric wears so well; it is "all of a piece," and "alike on both sides," the soul's most pleasant garment for all climates. Emerson calls companionship "the meeting of two in a thought," and adds: "What is so rare?"

Another test: Compare your hand with that of Sophroniscus next time he calls. It is not enough to be married down to the eyebrows; you must be married hand to hand. Now, has he one of those immense hands that could crush yours as if it were an egg-shell? Then you are not mated, and will pull like an ill-matched span through life. The firm, steady, even clasp of a pair of bread-winners ought to be realized when you obey the minister's instructions to "join hands" at the altar. If his idea is that of the Orientals, the Indians, and other semi-civilized men, that the more money he earns the more jewels you will hang on, then a true marriage can never be made by your respective hands. Whether you pursue a wage-earning avocation or not, you must have one, if you are a thoroughly self-respecting young person, or you are too immature to enter upon the sanctities of the married estate.

Another test: Do you keep step easily and naturally with Sophroniscus? It is the outward sign of an inward grace. Do you walk along, instinctively, to the same places—the church, the prayer-meeting, the temperance rally, the lyceum? Or, does he leave you a few minutes that he may "go and see a man"? Do you lean on him a good deal as you walk? The best every-day illustration of a true marriage is a well-matched team—I have just left Kentucky, so pardon the allusion. Can you hold your own in such a pairing? If not, you are "ower young to marry yet."

Charles V. tried to make two watches run just alike and failed. What shall we say of a similar attempt with two personalities, where you have the main-springs of variant reason, the balance-wheel of unmatched judgment, the fine jewels of unadjusted fancy and imagination, the dial-plate of human faces, and the pointers of character thereon? Other things being equal, the earlier the better for this intricate adjustment to begin. One of my famous doctors condenses the whole argument into these sententious words:

"In reply to your inquiry, I may state that I think the best age for marriage is twenty-five in the man and twenty in the woman. Their physical systems have then attained their full development, and their mental characteristics are still sufficiently flexible and plastic for that mutual accommodation which is one of the great spiritual uses of marriage."

The reciprocal attraction of two natures out of a thousand million for each other is the strongest but one of the most unnoted proofs of a beneficent Creator. It is the fairest, sweetest rose of time, whose petals and whose perfume expand so far that every one of us is inclosed and sheltered by their tenderness and beauty. For folded in its heart we find the germ of every home; of those beatitudes, motherhood, fatherhood, sisterly and brotherly love; the passion of the patriot, the calm and steadfast love of the philanthropist. Let the attuning of the twain whom God for noblest love hath made begin in childhood by a reform in the present denaturalizing methods of a civilization largely based on force, by which the boy and girl are sedulously trained apart. Set them side by side in school, in church, in government, as God has set male and female everywhere side by side throughout His realm of law, and has declared them one throughout His realm of grace. Fulfil the poet's prophecy about "two heads in counsel," as well as "two beside the hearth."

Train those with each other who were formed for each other. Let the American home with its method based upon natural law root out all that remains of the French, the Monastic, and the Harem philosophies concerning this greatest problem of all time. Then, when she is "of age," when she fulfils the tests here instituted, let woman who is chosen set herself to man (the man of *her* choice), "like perfect music unto noblest words."

CHAPTER XIII.

TO THE YOUNG WOMEN'S CHRISTIAN TEMPERANCE UNIONS— UNITY OF PURPOSE.

It is a law of dynamics, that if the projectile force be strong enough and the momentum sufficiently sustained, even a small body may gain percussive impetus enough to split a world in two. Summer lightning on the clouds is pleasant to look at, but chain lightning strikes. The great lakes flow along lazy and silent, but condensed at Niagara they roar like a perpetual cyclone. Coming to the point is the law of achievement. Scattered forces never win a battle; it is the pounding of compact forces on one spot that breaks the ranks and routs the foe. Scattered faculties are at the same disadvantage; they spread out thin; they compass nothing determinate. They are under the perpetual law: "Jack at all trades, but master of none."

But, *per contra*, the liquor traffic and the drink curse are undermining our civilization; all admit this in a general way, but only a few feel it like a fire in the bones. These must serve as storm signals to rouse the rest; as lightning-rods to draw the fire of public opinion; as voices crying in the wilderness. The fight for a clear brain is on; the troops deploying; there is no time to lose; let us devote our lives as Christians, patriots, defenders of the weak. There is brain-growth in it; there is heart-culture; there is victory—and all heaven afterward for beauty, poetry and love. John Howard declined an invitation to the Czar's dinner-table that he might visit one more noisome cell in St. Petersburg; Wesley knew no such word as rest from preaching, writing, and organizing the great gospel new departure of his time; Lord Brougham, when asked if he had read a popular new history, replied, "No; I am too busy making history myself;" Bishop Janes, attending conferences in the vicinity, never saw the Rhine or the "Sistine Madonna;" David Livingstone forswore every intellectual and social preference that he might probe that "open sore of the world," the slave trade; Bishop Taylor plunges into the heart of Africa with his fingers in his ears. What these heroic souls have felt on a grand scale, we may feel according to our power, in the high task to which God and America have called us. We shall be tempted to paths more flowery, called by voices more congenial. Sometimes our hearts may falter; sometimes we may not deal nobly, wisely, and lovingly with all. But we can pray for guidance; we can help each other by gentle admonition. So let us go forward steadily and without fear, renouncing much that we may gain still more, and clinging to the motto, "*Mea vita vota*," but remembering, as we move forward, that "a wise man on a crowded street winneth his way by gentleness."

CHAPTER XIV.

"FINALLY, SISTERS."

LAST of all, remember a Christian life is evermore a life of action. As my dear friend and cousin, Deacon Willard, says, "Head faith built Noah's Ark; heart faith went into it." Head faith amounts to little; heart faith sets the world on fire with love. Head faith looks, heart faith grasps. Suppose you put out a sign, "Bread for the hungry;" I might believe that sign, because I knew you were trustworthy and generous. That would be head faith, but it wouldn't feed me. Heart faith goes in, takes the bread, eats it, and satisfies its hunger. This is the age of hard facts. Christian living must be every-day business. We must be able to say in our fashion, what a converted Indian said in his: "No good for bad white man to tell me the Bible not true. It stopped my swearin', and stealin', and lyin', when I'd done 'em all forty years steady. It's a miracle that I've stopped, but it would be a bigger one if a book that wa'n't true could a made me."

Arm-chair Christianity won't pass muster nowadays. Soldiers of Him who went about doing good have something on hand besides murmuring:

> "My willing soul would stay
> In such a frame as this,
> And sit and sing herself away
> To everlasting bliss."

Look at the change in our hymns! "Rescue the Perishing," "Hold the Fort," "Let the Lower Lights be Burning"—these give the keynote to the grand army that is going forth to trample under foot the dragons of intemperance, impurity, and every other form of sin, in these stirring days of Gospel warfare. So, dear friend, "be not simply good, be good for something;" not a barnacle on the old ship Zion, but a gleaming, sun-bright sail; not a drone in the great hive of humanity, but a happy, humming, honey-gathering bee; not a croaker, but a persuasive voice. Thus shall it surely come to pass if now, henceforth, and always you go forward saying with your lips and by your life:

"Lead, kindly Light, amid the encircling gloom,
Lead thou me on!"

MISS ROSE ELIZABETH CLEVELAND'S BOOK.

"*GEORGE ELIOT'S POETRY AND OTHER STUDIES.*"
Square, 12mo, 191 pp., $1.50; Subscription Edition, with Portrait of Authoress, $2.00; gilt, $2.50.

Contents.

George Eliot's Poetry.
Reciprocity.
Altruistic Faith.
Charlemagne.
The Monastery.

Old Rome and New France.
Studies in the Middle Ages;
History.
Chivalry.
Joan of Arc.

Harriet Beecher Stowe says: "In my opinion it is a book of which all women may well be proud. Far from anything weak or sentimental, it is an expression of vigorous habits of thought, of high culture, of firm principle and earnest feeling, and, in short, it represents *the American woman at her best*. I rejoice to think that the White House has such a woman at its head."

George Parsons Lathrop says: "These essays are valuable for their quality of insight and earnest feeling. I am greatly pleased by her sincere womanly tone, and think that her presentation of historical episodes is calculated to arouse the imagination and impress readers vividly."

R. H. Stoddard, in the New York World, says: "Miss Cleveland's ideals are high, and her self-respect is great. The volume shows that she can be critical, and that she is able to form an independent opinion."

Charles A. Dana, Editor New York Sun, says: "Miss Cleveland's literary style is characterized by vigor of expression, abundance of imagery, and a certain rhythmic quality that makes passages here and there read almost like blank verse."

Edna Dean Proctor says: "Miss Cleveland's essay on George Eliot's Poetry is a piquant, far-reaching criticism, and in all her pages there is something of the freshness and force of the north wind."

FUNK & WAGNALLS, Publishers.

A NEW BOOK BY JOSIAH ALLEN'S WIFE.

SWEET CICELY.—A story of the Josiah Allen's Wife's Series. Of thrilling interest. Over 100 illustrations, 12mo, cloth, $2.00.

"Josiah Allen's Wife" has always been a shrewd observer of human nature as it reveals itself in the round of homely, every day life, and the keen sarcasm and adroit humor with which she lays bare its foibles, its weaknesses and its grotesque outcroppings has rarely, if ever, been equaled. The strong feature of all Miss Holley's humor, is its moral tone. The present work will treat the "temperance sentiment" in new phase—that of a semi-humorous novel.

SOME OPINIONS OF "JOSIAH ALLEN'S WIFE":

The Woman's Journal, Boston: "The keen sarcasm, cheerful wit and cogent arguments of her books have convinced thousands of the 'folly of their ways,' for wit can pierce where grave counsel fails."

The Herald, New York: "Her fun is not far-fetched, but easy and spontaneous. She is now witty, now pathetic, yet ever strikingly original."

The Home Journal, New York: "She is one of the most original humorists of the day."

The New Era, Lancaster, Pa.: "Undoubtedly one of the truest humorists. Nothing short of a cast-iron man can resist the exquisite, droll and contagious mirth of her writings."

FUNK & WAGNALLS,   New York.

TWO NEW NOVELS BY JULIAN HAWTHORNE.

"*THE COUNTESS ALMARA'S MURDER*" and "*THE TRIAL OF GIDEON.*" Both bound in one volume, cloth, 75 cts. To be ready about June 20th.

The plot of the first novel is laid in prehistoric times on the hills of Moab; that of the second in New York City. Julian Hawthorne is a writer of remarkable ability. No living writer equals him in the creative power of imagination. Take what subject he will, Mr. Hawthorne always throws around it the glamour of a charming literary style, and exhibits, even in his lightest writings, the color of a thoughtful and brilliant mind. His style is exceedingly fascinating.

WHAT THE CRITICS SAY OF JULIAN HAWTHORNE.

The Independent, New York, says: "Julian Hawthorne can choose no better compliment upon his new romance (Archibald Malmaison) than the assurance that he has at last put forth a story which reads as if the manuscript, written in his father's indecipherable handwriting and signed 'Nathaniel Hawthorne,' had lain shut into a desk for 25 years, to be only just now pulled out and printed. It is a masterful romance; short, compressed, and terribly dramatic."

The London Times says: "After perusal of this weird, fantastic tale (Archibald Malmaison), it must be admitted that upon the shoulders of Julian Hawthorne has descended the mantle of his illustrious father. The climax is so terrible, and so dramatic in its intensity, that it is impossible to class it with any situation of modern fiction."

FUNK & WAGNALLS, Publishers.

THE HOYT-WARD CYCLOPÆDIA OF PRACTICAL QUOTATIONS.

Prose and Poetry. Nearly 20,000 Quotations and 50,000 lines of Concordance.

It contains the celebrated quotations and all the useful Proverbs and Mottoes from the English, Latin, French, German, Italian, Spanish and Portuguese, classified according to subjects. Latin Law Terms and Phrases, Legal Maxims, etc. (all with translations).

It has a vast concordance of nearly 50,000 lines, by which any quotation of note may at once be found and traced to its source. It is to quotations what Young's or Cruden's Concordance is to the Bible.

Its Table of Contents: Index of Authors, giving date of birth, nativity, etc.; Topical Index with Cross References, Index of Subjects, Index of Translation, together with its immense Concordance and many other features desirable in a work of reference, combine to make this Cyclopædia what it is.

THE ONLY STANDARD BOOK OF QUOTATIONS.

Invaluable to the Statesman, Lawyer Editor, Public Speaker, Teacher or General Reader.

NOAH PORTER, D.D., LL.D., Pres. Yale College. "It will be a help and a pleasure to many."

HON. SAMUEL J. RANDALL, WASHINGTON. "The best book of quotations which I have seen."

GEO. F. EDMUNDS, U. S. SENATOR. "It is the most complete and best work of the kind with which I am acquainted."

HON. ABRAM S. HEWITT. "The completeness of its indices is simply astonishing."

HON. F. T. FRELINGHUYSEN, Secretary of State. "Am much pleased with the Cyclopædia of Quotations."

HENRY WARD BEECHER. "Good all the way through, especially the proverbs of all nations."

HENRY W. LONGFELLOW. "Can hardly fail to be a very successful and favorite volume."

WENDELL PHILLIPS. "Its variety and fullness and the completeness of its index gives it rare value to the scholar."

Royal octavo, over 900 pp. Cloth, $5.00; Sheep, $6.50; Fancy Cloth, Extra Gilt, $7.50; Half Morocco, Gilt, $8.00; Full Morocco, Extra Finish and Gilt, $10.00.

FUNK & WAGNALLS, Publishers,   **N. Y.**

www.ingramcontent.com/pod-product-compliance
Lightning Source LLC
Chambersburg PA
CBHW031345160426
43196CB00007B/741